Color Struck

Pamela & Joel Tuck

Joechel Books

www.pamelamtuck.com

Place orders at:
www.pamelamtuck.com

Acknowledgment

We give our sincere thanks to Grandma Doll for sharing her story. Her faith and integrity not only touched the lives of her immediate family, but also the lives of those who learned of her.

Although this story is based on real life experiences, many names, identifying characteristics, and events have been changed or altered for privacy protection.

Chapter 1

The Division

"A deathbed shouldn't be the peacemaker in this family." Pa-Pa preached that to us like it was a promise we had to keep. He said, "It'll be too late for y'all to wait 'til you're dying, before you show love for one another. I don't want to see this family go through that...never again."

I didn't understand what he meant—just took it as old folks talk. I wished I had asked more questions, especially when I started seeing tension between my two older cousins. I would have never thought skin color would cause a division between us. It was too late for Pa-Pa to explain his teachings—he was gone.

****

My stomach had a nervous twitch, as I stood at Grandma's kitchen window. Pat dashed across the yard. She wore her favorite sweatshirt, displaying Africa in a raised leather design of red, black, and green. The word *MOTHERLAND* was written in gold glitter and stretched across her broad shoulders.

She rushed in, with a gush of cool air following her.

"Good morning," she said in unison with the *bang* of the screen door.

"Morning, baby," Grandma replied. "What did I tell you 'bout letting my door slam like that? Close it easy, child."

"Sorry, Grandma, but that was the wind."

"It's that strong out there?"

"Yes, ma'am, it looks like a storm's coming."

Pat dropped her backpack by the door and joined me at the window, just in time to see Cherie strutting across the yard. She was walking toward the end of the path where we caught the bus. She never turned in our direction—just stood outside, with her arms folded and her back to us.

"With all that *brain*, you'd think she'd have more common sense," Pat said. "Supposed to be setting an example."

"I'm telling you," I agreed. "Can't she tell a storm's coming?"

"Maybe it'll blow her away," Pat said, bumping me on the arm.

"Yeah, and bring back the old Cherie," I added.

We both burst into sly giggles.

Grandma was busy humming, until she heard us snickering. "You girls are mighty tickled this morning for some reason." Her eyes shifted to the clock on the wall; she frowned. "Where's Cherie? She should've been here by now. Is she sick today?"

"Yes, ma'am, she's sick all right," Pat started, "sick in that high-minded head of hers."

"What are you talking 'bout, child?"

"She's outside, Grandma," Pat continued. "She probably didn't come in to speak to you because you're fixing salmon and eggs."

Grandma's back stiffened.

"The last time you fixed it, she complained about her clothes smelling fishy," Pat said. "You know, uppity folks eat bacon and eggs for breakfast, not fish and eggs."

Grandma slowly crossed her arms into a tight fold, the corners of her lips dipped downward, and her nostrils flared to their full width to finalize the peak of her aggravation. "You mean to tell me she'd rather stand outside, 'cause of what I'm cooking? Humph, foolish thing. Tell that child to get in here."

Pat rushed out the door. She was on a mission. I followed her onto the porch—just in case I was needed.

She stood in front of Cherie with her hands on her

hips. Her head swayed from side to side, like a waddling duck. "I don't know why you're standing out here like somebody crazy."

"There's a lot you don't know. And furthermore, what I do is *my* business."

"I could care less about what you do," Pat said, dropping her hands to her side.

"Then why are you antagonizing me?"

"There you go with your big words—probably don't even know what it means."

"Small words are for small brains," Cherie said.

"Girl, please. Your fancy talk doesn't change where you came from," Pat said, clenching her fists tight.

"Get out of my—"

"Grandma said come in the house!" I shouted.

They turned toward me. I knew I had to distract them before something worse happened. It seemed like they were always fussing. I didn't like Cherie's new attitude either, but I tried to ignore it—Pat challenged it in every way possible.

Cherie sucked her teeth, rolled her eyes, and took one last look down the road. When she didn't see any sign of the bus, she threw her head in the air and swirled around like a top. It seemed to me that she wanted her backpack to *whack* Pat right in those poked-out lips of hers. Then she stormed right past me like I wasn't even there.

She jerked when she opened the kitchen door. *Did the smell smack her that hard?* If so, I couldn't half blame her. That salmon sure is a strong smelling fish, especially when pan-fried with onions. I guess I never thought too much about it, not until Cherie started cutting up.

We were right on her heels—she hesitated—eased her head into the kitchen, without exposing her clothes.

"Yes, Grandma, did you summon me?"

"Summon? I ain't got time for your proper talk, child. You ain't got no business out there, with a storm coming."

"I thought I heard the bus."

"You ain't heard no bus," Grandma said. "Get in this house before you catch your death."

Cherie slowly pulled herself inside. Pat bumped past her with a victory stride. I followed.

I felt sorry for Cherie, but I couldn't help but giggle when I noticed how close she stood in front of the screen door. My only thought was that she was trying to let the draft air out the strong smells that were seeping steadily into her clothes.

Grandma seemed completely satisfied. She went back to humming and pulled her golden biscuits out of the oven. The air had a mixture of salmon, onions, and butter all blended so richly; my stomach started rumbling.

"Y'all ready for something to eat?" Grandma said, with pure delight glowing from her face. "You need a hearty breakfast to get your lessons out good."

"Yes, ma'am," Pat and I answered together.

"No thanks," Cherie said, rotating in the draft. "I ate before I left home."

Pat gave her a disgusted look. "You're too good to eat at Grandma's now?"

"I said I ate before I left home. Obviously, I'm not hungry," Cherie said.

"No, what's obvious is your snobby attitude," Pat said.

"You're one to talk about attitude."

"Y'all stop," Grandma said. "She ain't got to eat here if she don't want to."

Pat and I sat down at the table and went to work. I didn't understand what was going on with Cherie. She knew Grandma looked forward to feeding us on school mornings. We had always met there, ever since elementary school.

Grandma's house was in the middle, and ours formed a semi-circle around hers. Her house was the meeting place for the whole family: to gather, eat, discuss our problems, or just socialize. Things didn't seem so natural anymore.

Oh well, Grandma didn't seem a bit bothered by Cherie's funny ways. I tried to make up for them by starting little unnecessary conversations.

"Grandma, may I take some of your biscuits on the

bus? I love it when everybody begs for them."

Grandma's face shone with pride, but it seemed like she tried to be humble. "Say what? Them chil'ren want some of my biscuits? Um, um, um."

She shook her head, as if in disbelief, but I noticed her eagerly bagging biscuits.

It wasn't long before we heard the bus' horn blow at Cynthia's house—only one stop from us. Cherie was the first one out the door.

"Bye, Grandma," she said, as she ran to the edge of the path.

Pat and I grabbed our books and thanked Grandma for the breakfast. I took a handful of napkins and the bag of biscuits.

As I stepped on the bus, I handed our driver, Tyrone, a few. He squealed. "Thank you, Renee. I just love your grandmama's cookin'. Don't allow no eating on the bus, but this here is an exception."

When we were seated, that ole trouble-making Anthony Parker started teasing. "Fresh fish, fresh fish. Come and get your fish from the Steele's Fish Market."

All the kids burst out laughing. I never knew what to do in situations like that, so I just laughed, too. I noticed Cherie sitting as straight as an arrow, with her nose stuck in the air. It seemed like her Steele pride had her hypnotized into an intense gaze.

On the other hand, Pat, always the one with the mouth, spoke out on our behalf. "You're one to talk, Anthony. Smells like you had chit'lins for breakfast."

I knew Pat would stop his mouth, but I didn't know she would make it drop—low *ooohs* swept across the bus.

I just looked down at my bag, hoping no trouble would break out. I sure didn't feel like fighting that morning. Pa-Pa always said that we Steeles had to stick together—no matter what.

Tyrone must have felt the same way I did. "Ant, Pat, y'all cut it out before somebody starts passing licks," he said, with biscuit crumbs flying from his mouth.

Everything quieted down. I could still feel tension in the air. I wouldn't dare look up; I didn't want to meet those angry eyes of Anthony.

Somebody started a conversation in the back of the bus. Boy, was I relieved.

The warm, buttery smell drifted out of my bag and reminded me of my purpose for having it. It wasn't long before a back seat voice inquired, "Renee, you got any more of those biscuits?"

****

It was hard to concentrate in my classes. I kept meditating on what had happened at Grandma's. I wished there was something I could do to make things right between Cherie and Pat. Their clashing attitudes were tearing my world apart.

I was glad to hear the bell for lunch. I fused with the students filling the halls with commotion. I ignored the bumps and pushes of the people rushing past me. Their conversations were at a distance, as I walked in a daze.

I felt a sharp tap on my shoulder. It was Pat. "Hey, girl, glad I caught up with you. Didn't you hear me call you?"

"No, I guess my mind was on other things."

"Oh, you had me worried there for a minute—didn't know if you were turning into another Cherie," she joked. "Listen, do you have any extra money? I forgot my wallet."

We stopped in the commons area, outside the cafeteria. I checked my purse. "I don't think I have enough."

Pat spotted Cherie walking toward the cafeteria with her friends. "She really gets to me," she said, sucking her teeth.

It grieved me to see Cherie laughing, talking, and falling into her friends—her new family. I longed to be with her, too.

"Let's go ask Cherie," I said. "I'm pretty sure she has enough money."

One look at Pat told me how dumb I sounded.

"I don't want to ask her for nothing," she said. "I'll starve first."

"Well, I'll go."

I ran into the cafeteria. Cherie and her friends clustered at the end of the line. Her back was to me.

"Cherie!"

She turned in my direction.

"I need to talk to you. It's real important," I said, motioning for her to come over.

She turned back to her friends; I felt invisible.

"Cherie!" I said, pleading.

She never turned around again. I felt sick. I ran past Pat and headed for the bathroom. In seconds, Pat burst through the door.

"What's wrong with you, Renee?"

I splashed cold water on my face to soothe the stinging in my eyes. I couldn't answer because of the lump in my throat.

"It's Cherie isn't it? I don't know why you even try."

"She's so different," I said, choking back the tears.

"She's forgetting who she is. Don't worry about her."

"I'm not hungry," I said, drying my face with a paper towel. "Just take my money and get yourself some lunch."

"If you don't eat, I don't eat," Pat said. "Some of us Steeles have to stick together."

Pat hugged me tight. I was swallowed up by soft fleece, as my face pressed against the warm leather on her sweatshirt. I cried on the *motherland*.

****

On Fridays, we always waited at Grandma's house until the rest of the family got home from work. It seemed like that school day was never going to end.

Pat and Cherie had nothing to say to one another on the ride home. I didn't see how those girls could hold grudges for so long. One was just as stubborn as the other.

Cherie, being the oldest at seventeen, acted as if we should've looked up to her. She was going to be the first grandchild to graduate. I guess that's why she tried to set a good example with her elaborate speech and college dreams. Delicate features accented her soft yellow complexion: naturally arched eyebrows, slender nose, and heart-shaped lips all influenced the prim and properness she displayed. Regardless of her small build, she had a strong Steele determination.

Pat, on the other hand, *wasn't gonna be second to nobody,* and had to have the last word. Her chocolate colored complexion blended with the boldness of her personality. Thick eyebrows, high cheekbones, and full lips added richness to her African features. She flaunted her broad build with little intimidation to anybody or anything. She was determined to leave an impression of her heritage wherever she went.

I looked up to both of them, even though I was still trying to find myself and the statement I needed to make. My caramel colored skin was just another reminder of how I was torn between the two of them. Our differences never seemed to matter before. That's why I had to think of some way to fix the problems between them...*but how? That was another issue to discuss at Grandma's. She always knew how to handle things.*

"Renee, you plan to stay on the bus the whole weekend?" Tyrone yelled, breaking my thoughts. "Go ahead and get off, so you can bring me some more of them biscuits on Monday."

I grabbed my backpack and ran to the front of the bus. "Sorry, Tyrone, lost in thought."

"That's all right. Don't forget to thank your grandmama for me."

****

The stress rolled off my shoulders, as the coziness of Grandma's house greeted me.

Her home was nothing extravagant, having a radio as its only medium to the outside world. Even that was limited solely to retrieving the time, temperature or listening to her pastor on Sunday mornings. Except for us, Grandma completely separated herself from the world and the things of the world, as she would say.

Regardless of the quaintness of her home, it held the same peacefulness she possessed. The well-kept, antique furniture must have been over a hundred years old. Grandma always made sure it was shiny enough to see herself in it; I never seen a speck of dust around. The knotty pine walls grasped the rustic look, and their coat of shellac, applied by our daddies, complemented the immaculate glow of the house.

I believed Grandma cherished her home because Pa-Pa built it for her back in the early sixties. I could tell he had her in mind when he built it, not holding back on the nooks and crannies she adored.

Precious memories of him swept through every corner of the house. A warm sense of security embraced me whenever I entered.

It seemed like Pat felt the same relief Grandma's house offered.

"I hate having to do homework over the weekend. It just interferes with my plans," she said, dropping her backpack to the floor with a loud, *thud.*

"Proper application of yourself would allow you to have more recreational time," Cherie sarcastically remarked.

"Oh, Miss Proper got all the answers," Pat replied with a British accent.

"Perhaps if you pursued more answers, you may increase your slim chances of going to college," Cherie said.

"I'm sick of your—"

"Girls, I ain't gonna have this carrying on morning and evening," Grandma said, frowning. "If you ain't got nothing good to say, then don't say nothing."

I tried to ease the tension. "What are you doing, Grandma?"

"Chopping slaw, baby," she said, as her face softened. "You know I always cook fish on Fridays. It won't seem right without the slaw."

I nodded, as I had known that for years.

"Your Uncle Leroy caught these here spots and

croakers back during the spring, at that James River Pier," Grandma continued. "I decided to take 'em out of the freezer and fry 'em."

She paused in her chopping. "I just put a pineapple scratch cake in the oven, too. The fambly ought to really enjoy themselves tonight."

"Cherie might want to stand outside once you start frying 'em, seeing that the house will smell like fish and all," Pat said.

Cherie ignored her and went to the buffet, where Grandma kept the family's mail.

"Grandma, have you seen anything for me? I sent away for some information from North Carolina State University."

"Naw, baby, I ain't seen nothing yet. Where's that school at?"

"It's in Raleigh, only about two hours from Greenville. They have a strong engineering program."

"Yeah, and it's a predominately white school," Pat added.

"So what? That's completely irrelevant. I have an academic interest and do not concern myself with the ratio of students who attend," Cherie said, looking up from her mail shuffling. "Besides, according to my research, their reputation excels other schools in North Carolina."

"Yeah, right," Pat said. "Did your research include the reputation of Shaw or A and T? You know, *black* schools."

Grandma seemed to have reached her limit with both girls. "Listen here, girls, y'all are first cousins and you're acting like irritated sitting hens. Ever since y'all started that high school, y'all been pulled apart. What ails you?"

"Well, Grandma," Pat started, in a more humble tone, "Cherie used to be all right until she started those honor classes and hanging with her *light-skinned* friends."

"Grandma, I'm preparing myself for higher education," Cherie said. "I don't want to stay in the country all my life. I associate with people who are more like me."

Grandma gave Cherie a grave look. "What do you

mean *like* you?"

"W-Well…I-I mean…you know…people with the same interests."

"So you mean to tell me that only your friends have the same interests as you?"

"Of course not. It's just that we all have the same classes and—"

"Cherie, you pick and choose who you want to hang with and you know it," Pat said. "You hang with Nicole and Monica and they repeated tenth grade—they're in two of my classes."

"Well…um," Cherie began, "I've known them awhile."

"You've known us all your life, and you disown me and Renee. I guess we ain't light enough for you, huh?"

Grandma looked completely shocked. "What do you mean she disowns you and Renee?"

"When she's with her friends, who are all light-skinned like her, she turns her head when she sees us," Pat said. "She did it today and had Renee crying."

I felt the heat rise to my cheeks. *Why did Pat have to tell that?*

Grandma searched my face. "Is that right, Renee?"

I hated to be torn in the middle, but I couldn't lie to Grandma. I couldn't bring myself to speak; I nodded.

Grandma propped her hands on her hips and her face transformed completely: eyebrows unevenly cocked and cheeks slightly puffed, pushing her lips into a pouting fashion.

"What kind of foolishness is this—you got a problem with color, child?"

"No, ma'am—"

"Yes she does, Grandma," Pat began, "I don't think she has any dark-skinned friends. The darker my friends are the better I like 'em."

"Well, you ain't no wise better, Pat," Grandma said, casting a mean eye at her. "Matter of fact, you're just as bad."

Pat dropped her head at Grandma's surprising statement. Grandma shot a dreadful look from Pat to Cherie and back again. None of my unnecessary conversations could penetrate through the tension.

Finally, her voice sliced through, "What's the cause of you treating your cousins like that, Cherie?"

"W-Well...I hardly see them...and...I-I'm trying to make friends with...with good connections...you know...when in Rome, you do as the Romans do."

"Child, let me tell you something. You ain't in no Rome—you're in Greenville, North Carolina, born in the country, just like the rest of us."

Grandma slowly shook her head from side to side, in a way as meaningful as a rattlesnake giving warning—she seemed as mad as one, as her eyes targeted Cherie.

"I think it's 'bout time I told y'all something I didn't share with you when your Pa-Pa was alive, out of due respect to him. But seeing what y'all done start doing, time is come for y'all to know some things, before y'all tear this fambly apart."

The impact of Grandma's words stirred a fearful curiosity.

"Y'all go in the den and wait for me. I got to finish chopping this slaw and put it in the Kelvinator, so it'll be ready by six o'clock. And I don't want to hear no more fussing, understand?"

"Yes, ma'am," Cherie and Pat answered in unison.

My voice finally returned to me. "Grandma, is there something I can help you do?"

"Naw, baby, I don't need no young hands in my old recipes. Just go sit with your cousins and try to keep peace like you always do."

When I entered the den, I noticed Cherie and Pat sat on opposite sides of the room, looking at their hands. They reminded me of students waiting for the principal.

I started one of my unnecessary conversations. "Grandma's got a lot of old stories. I can't imagine what she's been keeping from us all these years."

"Yeah, but there's a reason she kept this one," Cherie replied.

"Yeah, I know. That's what so scary," Pat said. "I hate making Grandma mad. I feel like God is gonna do something to me."

Cherie and I burst out laughing.

"Pat, as tough as you act sometimes, you ain't nothing but a big puff of wind," I said, chuckling.

"Don't try to put it all on me," Pat said, joining us in the giggling. "Y'all know y'all feel the same way."

"Yep," Cherie and I replied.

We filled the room with a pleasant laughter, something we hadn't heard between the three of us in a long time.

"Now, that's what I like to hear—fambly laughing and talking with each other," Grandma yelled from the kitchen. "I'll be there in just a minute."

Finally, we heard the refrigerator door open and close. Grandma walked into the den and sat down in her old rocker by the fireplace. She cupped her hands in the folds of her flour-dusted apron, and told us to gather around her.

Cherie and Pat must have forgotten about being mad at each other. They pulled their chairs beside one another, and left a tiny space for me to squeeze between them. We all looked at Grandma like baby birds waiting for whatever was about to drop out of her mouth.

Grandma looked at each one of us, as if she was searching our thoughts. She began speaking as softly as a mother reading a bedtime story. "Girls, y'all know that your Pa-Pa always wanted this fambly to stick together. He said ain't nobody gonna do for you like your fambly will."

We all nodded in agreement.

"But he won't raised that-a-way, and neither were his brothers or sisters. But 'cause of the tests and trials I had to go through with his fambly, that's something he learned. In turn, he wanted to teach it to y'all."

A sudden astonishment grasped my heart and made it sink into my stomach. *What did Grandma mean—Pa-Pa wasn't raised the way he had taught us all these years?* It seemed like Grandma heard my thoughts.

"There's a lot of hist'ry behind this here fambly, and a lot of hardships. I won't born a Steele, but I came to live up to that name. I was a Dupree, I was poor, and worst of all, my skin color was too dark. Them three things won't no good combination for your great-grandpa Steele."

Cherie, Pat, and I shot glances at each other.

"Nevertheless, whether he liked it or not, I became a Steele just the same," Grandma continued. "And with the help of God, I survived to tell about it. It all started a long time ago, when my oldest sister, Lena, started courting."

As Grandma began her narrative, my mind opened to a time unknown to me, yet my curiosity welcomed it. I wasn't sure if I was ready for all that was in store—it was a challenge I was willing to take.

Chapter 2

Grandma's Story (Courtship)

Me, Lena, and Hattie were sort of like y'all—'bout one year apart. We were all courting age, but Lena, being the oldest at eighteen, was expected to be married first. Your Aunt Hattie was the youngest at sixteen, but she was bent and determined to be married, if it was the last thing she did. I guess ole Lena was taking too long for her.

'Long back then, folks didn't allow no courting by yourself. Whenever Lena had a fella visiting, me and Hattie had to be in the same room—keeping watch.

One day, we were washing clothes, and Lena was expecting company—a fella by the name of Johnny Ray. He was one character. It was a hot summer day in 1947. Me and Hattie were really feeling it.

"Tell you, Bell, it's sure 'nough scorching out here," Hattie said, wiping sweat from her forehead. "Seems though we ain't never gonna finish these clothes."

"It looks to be a few more pieces to hang up," I said. "But the ground's so dusty; I hope we don't have to rewash 'em."

"I sure hope not. I's got to get busy writing another hollow oak tree letter."

Me and Hattie know'd our Pa didn't want us to have no parts with them Steele boys, but Hattie had her heart set on your Uncle Amos. She was strong-headed—won't 'bout to let Pa stop her.

She and Amos had started leaving little notes for each other in the hollow of an old oak tree, near our house.

They had to wrap them letters in a piece of cut burlap and lay a rock on top—to make sure nothing got to it. Them two was right faithful. I couldn't see what they had so much to talk about. But every few days, Hattie unfolded a new letter to read before she went to bed.

I didn't have the guts she did, but I kind of had my heart set on your Pa-Pa 'long back then. He was Amos' cousin. They called him Buck. His daddy was the one Pa had the problem with—my chances were real slim.

I know'd Buck and Amos hung together; when you saw one, you saw the other. I decided I'd find out the progress Hattie was making.

"Have you heard anything from that Amos Steele lately?"

"Naw, ain't heard from him yet," Hattie said, sighing in a dreamy way. "That's why I's got to get to writing. Maybe I'll ask him to come pay me a visit one of these days—make sure I tell him to bring Buck 'long."

"Y-Y-You crazy? You know if Pa found out we wanted to court them boys, he'd near 'bout kill us."

Right 'long then, we heard Johnny Ray coming up the path, yelling at that ole bummed up mule of his.

Hattie had 'bout as much mouth as Pat; she didn't hold her tongue, either.

When she caught sight of Johnny Ray, she whispered, "Bell, speaking of courting, look at Johnny Ray slugging up here with that ole Samson. Looks like that mule's gonna topple over any minute—call hisself courtin' Lena."

Most of the time I hated to see him coming, but it was so hot that day, 'til I was kind of glad to see him. Ma was sure to come up with some kind of excuse to call us in. We tried to hurry and finish hanging the clothes.

Johnny Ray had one of the most stubborn mules I'd ever seen. When Samson started twitching them ears, you'd better look out—no telling which-a-way he'd take off.

Hattie was still eyeing Johnny Ray from between the clothes. "That Samson must be twitching them ears," she whispered. "Johnny Ray is justa kicking and he won't budge an inch. I sure hope he's got a good hold on that dumb mule."

No sooner than she got the words out of her mouth good, Samson done jerked and throwed Johnny Ray off like a dish rag.

Me and Hattie held the clothes up in front of our faces, so he wouldn't see us laughing. When we got ourselves together, we saw him scrambling—trying to dust hisself off. He looked around, I guess to see if anybody seen him.

Samson seemed to be satisfied with what he'd done, 'cause he let Johnny Ray get back on him. Then he walked just as easy, like he ain't done a thing.

Hattie hated that mule. She sure didn't want him near the house.

"Bell, we better tell Johnny Ray to tie Samson by that hollow oak tree before he ties him to the porch. Ought to have better sense, seeing we's got these clean clothes. That ole contrary mule'll kick dust all over ever'thing."

I know'd she was right. I took off down the path to meet Johnny Ray before he got too close.

"Hey, Bell, how ya doing?" he said, right lazy-like.

"Doing fine, Johnny Ray. Listen, me and Hattie were wondering if you could tie Samson to the hollow oak tree, 'cause we just hung out some clean clothes."

"Sure, no problem at all," he replied.

When he turned to take Samson back to the oak tree, I saw a big spot of dust on his breeches.

"Johnny Ray, look like you got a lil dust behind you," I said, trying to keep a straight face.

I couldn't hold myself for long. That tickle I had, when we seen him fall off Samson, came back and grabbed me, 'til I burst out laughing.

He looked right embarrassed. "Yeah, I know. That ole devilish, stubborn Samson—he got a mind of his own. He done throwed me. Guess I had my mind all tied up in Lena…won't paying attention to them ears of his…won't holding him tight enough."

He grabbed Samson by the reins. I finally got myself together, after being a little ashamed for laughing. I walked with him to the oak tree.

"Pa won't let me shoot him. I sure would like to though," he said, knocking dust off the back of his breeches. "Did I get ever'thing, Bell? You know I want to look my best before I see Lena."

"You look fine."

We headed toward the house.

"How ya doing today, Hattie?" Johnny Ray said, grinning from ear to ear.

"Fine," she said dryly.

He didn't seem to be bothered by Hattie's ways; just tipped his hat to us. "Y'all have a nice day now, ya hear?"

After he made his way into the house, Hattie nudged me. "Now he ought to know Lena ain't interested in him. As many fellas who come up here to see her—he's 'bout the dirtiest one of 'em all."

I felt right sorry for him. I know'd Hattie was right, but I kind of liked his easygoing way. I didn't want to speak against him.

"Yeah, Hattie, but that's her decision. We'd better get finished before Ma comes calling."

I was busy hanging clothes. Hattie just stood there with that ole dreamy look in her eyes. I didn't have to wonder long about what she was thinking.

"Sure would like for Amos and Buck to come visit us sometime. We wouldn't have to worry 'bout them being dusty, 'cause Buck got a car."

"You can hardly keep your mind off that Steele boy."

"Bell, you're one to talk. You know you got your eyes on Buck."

"They are some right handsome fellas, but ain't no need of us getting our hopes up. Ever since Pa had that falling out with Buck's daddy—"

"Bell, Hattie! Y'all 'bout finished out there?"

"Coming, Ma, just got a few more pieces," I replied.

****

Your Aunt Hattie didn't waste no time getting a letter to that hollow oak tree. She done just like she said she was. But instead of asking Amos to come to the house, she asked him to meet us at the little store—not far from home. Ma or Pa used to send us there on errands to fetch things they wanted.

'Bout a week or so after Hattie wrote her letter, she unfolded another one of them letters from Amos.

"Bell, guess what?"

She said it so quick, 'til I didn't know if somebody had died or what; I was scary-like anyhow.

"What's wrong?"

Hattie squealed like a stuck pig. She fell on the bed, folding her arms across her chest right tight.

"What ails you?" I asked, feeling the heat leave my body. She was too young to be having a heart attack.

She rolled 'round laughing and kicking. That's when I seen the letter in her hands.

"We's got to make it to the store this coming Saturday. Amos wants to meet me there. And Buck's coming 'long to see you."

Felt like my whole stomach fell down to my feet and left a weak shaking in my legs. I just stood there looking at Hattie with my mouth dropped open.

Hattie didn't pay me no mind. She swirled 'round the room 'til it almost made me dizzy watching her. She picked through her little rags, trying to find the most decent thing to wear. We didn't have much in the way of clothes. Just one Sunday-go-to-meeting dress for each girl, and a few old gingham dresses for 'round the house.

"What you think 'bout this one?" she said, holding up one of her better dresses. "Just needs a lil mending 'round the collar."

I couldn't say nothing right away—still shocked I guess.

"Ain't no need standing there looking right scared," she said, giving me a mean eye. "You better find yo'self something to wear."

"I don't think I'm gonna go. Buck probably ain't interested in me. And what if Pa finds out? Ain't no Steele boy worth that."

She came right near me. "Now, you listen here, Amos done told me Buck wants to see you. Now that there proves he interested in you. Pa's the one who got a problem with them Steeles, not us. It ain't right for us to give up what we want 'cause of him."

She moved closer. I could feel the heat from her breath. "You're going with me on Saturday, if I's got to drag you. Now get your dress ready."

I didn't have much choice. My heart did skip a little, knowing Buck wanted to see me—I started picking through my things.

****

Saturday morning, I woke up with a stomachache. It won't nothing I ate—just a bad case of nerves. They had me doubled over and feeling like I had to vomit. Hattie didn't pay that no mind. She yanked my covers off and pulled me from the bed. I guess she meant what she said about dragging me with her.

"Come on, Bell, I ain't got time for you to be laying 'round. I's got a fella to meet."

"I don't feel too good," I said, moaning. "You're gonna have to go without me."

"That's all in yo' mind. You'll feel better once you starts to moving."

Hattie left to fetch the tin tub we used to get washed up in. I heard the pump squeaking on the back porch. I know'd it wouldn't be long before I was ready, wearing my favorite blue dress.

Hattie grabbed Pa's list in a hurry—before Ma could ask us why we were all fancied up. I didn't have much time to think, just yanked behind her.

Mr. Wiley and Buck's daddy were the only colored folks that had a store in these parts 'long then. Mr. Wiley's store was much closer to us, so Pa would send us there— even before he and Mr. Silas Steele had a falling out.

On our way to the store, I started feeling right faint. My knees felt like they were gonna give away. I slowed down, 'til I plumb stopped.

"Bell, what you stopping for? You know we's got to meet them fellas at the store."

"I don't think I can go no further. You know if Pa finds out we're—"

"We's just 'bout grown. Pa can't bind us up forever. You done come this far, ain't no need to go chicken on me. We's in this thing together—just trust me, everything's gonna be all right," Hattie said, pulling me along.

I took a deep breath and started walking again—dragging behind her. We finally got closer to the store.

"Do you see their car?" I asked.

"Naw, just the Watson's mule, the Mitchell's mule, Mr. Logan's mule, and chil'ren playing in front of the store."

"The same ole folks, huh?" I said, feeling a lil better. "I guess they're sitting 'round talking 'bout hard times, as usual."

Colored folks didn't have much. A few of them tried to get some learning by talking to Mr. Wiley 'bout business. Mr. Silas Steele was so puffed up—folks said he couldn't keep a level head or his feet on the ground. Nobody tried to get no smarts from him.

Me and Hattie walked in. Everybody was sitting 'round Mr. Wiley. Them that didn't have chairs, flipped old crates into seats. Mr. Wiley acted just like some kind of king, with all his poor, lil servants at his feet.

"Hey, girls," he said, looking up at us. "Y'all came to get your daddy's special?"

The folks started snickering a little. 'Bout everybody know'd Pa's special.

"Mr. Wiley, you know Pa just loves them Vienna sausages, sardines, and soda crackers," Hattie said, batting her eyes.

Mr. Wiley chuckled so hard, 'til his gigantic belly shook up and down.

"Yeah, I know," he said, finally catching his breath, "and he's got to finish up with a grape soda and peanuts."

The folks roared with laughter. Mr. Wiley finally got hisself together. "Go on and start collecting your stuff, you know where everything's at."

While me and Hattie were gathering Pa's things, Mr. Wiley's whole attitude changed.

"Sounds like I hear a car coming up the road," he said. "That sure is strange."

He left the folks sitting at the table and moved closer to the window.

"Ain't that many folks got cars 'round here," he said.

Mr. Wiley had the whole store peeking out the window—he recognized the car.

"Good gracious alive, if it ain't them Steele boys," he said. "Now what're they doing coming up here...seeing Silas got a store and all...reckon they come 'round here to spy."

My stomach dropped. Hattie's eyes were shining like new marbles. I guess she know'd 'bout how I felt—she nudged me.

"Bell, get yo'self together, here's our chance."

After a little bit, Amos and Buck walked in.

"How're you doing, Mr. Wiley, suh?" Buck said, nodding.

They were the most proper talking fellas, and right mannerly acting, too.

"Doing fine," Mr. Wiley said. "It's mighty strange for y'all to be in these parts this time of the day. You should still be at Silas' store working."

"Yes, suh, I know," Buck replied, "but we closed a little early, so we decided to stop by."

"You know good and well that y'all don't usually stop by, closing early or not. What's the *real* reason y'all came—yo' daddy sent you 'round here to check up on me?"

It seemed like you could almost hear a feather drop. Everybody was looking right at Mr. Wiley, Buck, and Amos. For that reason, I didn't mind looking, too.

Buck replied right easy-like, "Believe me, Mr. Wiley, what I come here for ain't got nothing to do with my daddy. But I did come for something in your store."

Buck looked over in our direction and nodded. I

could tell Mr. Wiley understood why they had come. He didn't look a bit pleased.

Finally, he broke the silence. "I don't want no foolishness from you boys. Y'all can look around if you want, but I'm gonna keep my eyes on you."

"Thank you, suh," Buck and Amos replied.

Hattie gave Amos one of her phony smiles that she had practiced. He fell for it and made his way over to us.

"How y'all doing today, girls?" Amos said. "Sure is nice seeing y'all again."

Hattie was still smiling like her mouth had gotten stuck. "We's doing fine. It's good seeing y'all, too. Thank you for making the trip."

"T'was my pleasure, Hattie, especially to see your pretty little face," he said.

She gave a shy laugh and went to sit with him at a little table by the wall—away from everybody else. There I was, standing with Buck. I couldn't think of nothing better to do than to look down at my feet.

"Speaking of pretty little faces, I wouldn't mind seeing yours," Buck said in a playful way. "I reckon I'd better get on the floor, so you'll speak to me."

I felt right embarrassed at myself. I looked up and gave a shaky smile. I didn't practice like Hattie did, so mine probably looked more like I was 'bout ready to cry—sure felt like it.

Buck had a way about him to make things feel comfortable though.

"There she is—Miss Lula Bell Dupree," he said, lifting up my chin. You look mighty fine in that blue dress."

"Thank you," I whispered.

He kept running his mouth. I guess trying to make me warm up a little. I could only nod. I was more interested in the talking going on behind him. I could tell Mr. Wiley didn't care for them boys coming up to his store to see us.

Buck couldn't get much talk out of me, so he offered to buy me a soda and Nabs. I had to answer one way or the other—I figured I might as well say *yes*. We didn't get sodas and peanut butter crackers too often.

Buck went to the counter and pulled out the biggest wad of money I'd ever seen in my whole life. It must have surprised Mr. Wiley, too, 'cause his eyes popped like they were gonna come clean out of his head. Everybody's mouths dropped wide open.

Mr. Wiley managed to close them huge jaws of his. "Now you mean to tell me, yo' daddy's doing that kind of business?"

"Yes, suh," Buck replied, smiling.

After paying for the sodas and Nabs, Buck talked real low to Mr. Wiley—so no ones could hear. The folds in Mr. Wiley's stout neck separated and bunched real slow, as he nodded to what Buck was saying. Buck slipped something to Mr. Wiley that made his face light up. His chubby fingers clutched it tight.

Mr. Wiley was a big man—seemed like it took all the energy in the world for him to move one foot before the other. But as soon as Buck made his way over to me, Mr. Wiley wobbled from behind the counter quick. All his limbs looked like they went into spasms—never know'd a person's body could move in so many different directions at once. He headed over to the table where the other folks were sitting and passed out money.

"Bell, you mind if we join Amos and Hattie at that table over there?" Buck said, breaking my stare.

I smiled and started walking. Me and Buck stopped by the counter to grab the sodas and Nabs.

I couldn't help but notice all the carrying on at the other tables—folks hovering and whispering. They reminded me of dogs in a meat house.

When we sat down, Buck leaned over the table. "I paid Mr. Wiley and these folks, so they won't tell y'alls daddy 'bout us meeting here."

Mr. Wiley's store was our meeting place every Saturday—for a while, anyhow.

****

It took me some time to build up my nerves, but I looked forward to meeting at the store. We met there for weeks.

Pa noticed how we were taking longer and longer to get home. "Why in the world do it take y'all gals so long to get home? All you're doing is going up the road a piece."

I was speechless. Hattie came up with some kind of excuse—enough to get us out of trouble.

Pa's curiosity bothered me. "Hattie, we better watch our time."

"You ain't nothing but a bundle of nerves, girl," she said. "Pa believes most anything I say." At least that's what she thought.

One Saturday at the store, me and Hattie were so wrapped up in talking, 'til we didn't hear the door open. Our backs were to it. Buck looked up. Fear jumped on his face. A real familiar voice spoke to Mr. Wiley. It seemed like everybody stopped breathing.

Me and Hattie spun our heads 'round like hoot owls. The tiny black slits in Pa's fierce eyes seemed to bore holes right through me. He didn't say a word—his look was as bad as a slap. Pa turned around and walked out.

Me and Hattie jumped up and followed him. We didn't say *bye* to Buck, Amos, Mr. Wiley or nobody. We were so scared that we even forgot to grab the bag with Pa's special in it. The worst part was that Pa wouldn't turn around to say a thing—just marched ahead with hard, wide steps.

When we reached the house, he laid right into us. "Here I am waiting and waiting all this time, and y'all at the store talking. And of all peoples, to them no good Steele boys."

Me and Hattie didn't open our mouths.

Pa kept blasting. "Let me tell y'all gals something. If I ever hear tell of y'all talking to them boys again, y'all gonna sure 'nough find yo'self outside looking in."

Hattie had courage to speak. "But we's just 'bout old as Lena, and you allow her to court."

"Don't you go sassing me, gal. Lena courts in a

respectful way, not behind my back. Them boys probably put y'all up to this here sneaking 'round. They're the last ones I want to see any one of my gals with."

I finally got enough heart to speak. "But why, Pa? They ain't done nothing to us."

I was always Pa's favorite, and he know'd that I was the quiet one; he calmed down a notch.

"Bell, let me tell you something 'bout that Silas Steele. He always had a little mo' than the rest of us colored folks 'round here, and he's right proud 'bout that. He thinks he can buy anybody and make 'em do just what he want 'em to...rumor has it, that's how he got that high-yella wife of his."

I didn't understand what Pa meant—I wouldn't dare interrupt him.

"Always had been funny 'bout color," Pa continued, "but enough about that. My problem with him gots to do with my oldest brother, Charlie."

Pa's face tightened. "Your Uncle Charlie was real bad off sick, and by me working on the white man's farm, I couldn't go and come like I pleased—could only get by to see him on Sundays."

Pa looked at us with sorrowful eyes, like he was begging for sympathy.

"His gal, Tina, was taking care of him by herself, and they lived closer to Silas' neck of the woods. He got word of Charlie being sick—know'd Tina was there struggling by herself. He took it upon hisself to help her; gave her money, food, and whatever else she mighta needed. Looked like a right nice gesture at first. But me and him had our differences on church beliefs; we never was able to set horses with each other. Nevertheless, he was helping my brother; I was thankful for that."

Pa paused, as if he had to brace hisself for his next words. "Your Uncle Charlie started getting worser, and with the way I was working, I couldn't get by there sometimes at all. Well...one day...Charlie died. And that good for nothing, Silas Steele, had made things right convenient for hisself by helping my niece—she felt like she owed him. He told Tina not to tell me 'bout her daddy being dead. Told her to go 'head and bury my brother without even letting me know. He claimed I didn't care 'bout my own brother, 'cause I hardly came by. He done all that stuff for her, and she felt like she had to do what he said."

Fury rekindled in Pa's eyes. "That gal buried Charlie. By the time I got 'round to see him, he had been in the ground 'bout three or four days."

Pa clenched his fist and swung it in the air. "Gals, I was so hurt and mad, I couldn't see straight. I didn't fault Tina, 'cause I know'd how Silas was—just as evil as a snake. I know'd won't no point in me saying nothing to him, 'cause I might of lost my religion; won't no reasoning with him no ways."

Pa unclenched his fist and pointed a mean finger at me and Hattie. "Now there's a saying 'bout the fruit don't fall far from the tree, so I'd 'spect that ole son and nephew of his ain't no wise better. That's the reason I don't want y'all talking to them boys. He done stole my brother from me—I ain't intending for him to take nothing else of mines away."

Me and Hattie just stood there in disbelief. I wouldn't think Buck's daddy would do something like that, but Pa wouldn't lie. I could see the hurt swell up in his eyes. He jerked away from us and stormed out of the house—leaving us standing there to swallow them bitter words.

Chapter 3

Aunt Jean Arrives

Grandma's kitchen door squeaked and banged, as Aunt Jean came in. "Mama, you got it smelling mighty good in here. Where're you at?"

"In the den with the girls...oh, I almost forgot about my cake. Don't walk so heavy, Jean," Grandma said, hurrying into the kitchen.

Cherie, Pat, and I loved our Aunt Jean, but she had the worst timing.

"Just when things were getting good," Pat said, sucking her teeth.

"I know," Cherie agreed, "I hope Aunt Jean doesn't talk long."

It was good hearing Cherie and Pat talk sensibly to each other.

"Maybe she'll join us, then Grandma can finish," I added.

Grandma came back into the den, with the smell of pineapple cake following her. She settled into her rocker. We heard Aunt Jean flipping through the mail—we sat, impatiently, waiting for her.

Finally, she headed toward the den. The light from the kitchen slowly smothered from sight—Aunt Jean *filled* the entrance. She stood there, greeting us with her bubbly, gapped-tooth smile, and wearing her awkward attire.

The *Just My Size* sweatshirt draped over her massive stomach, and though it took on unusual folds and creases, it still gave a comfortable look. Her freshly starched, pleated skirt, stopping just below her knocked knees, was a drastic offset to the sweatshirt—formal. To finish off her *costume*, she wore sneakers with soles that kissed the floor at inward angles, and striped bobby socks that looked as if they were saying *help us*, as they stretched around her pudgy ankles. Aunt Jean's clothing was a dead give away to the change she had undergone.

Grandma didn't believe in women wearing men's apparel—she even showed us where the Bible said it was an abomination. Although she allowed us to make our own decisions regarding religion, she refused to compromise her beliefs, which resulted in us conforming to her ways. We abided by her wishes by wearing either dresses or skirts whenever we came over. In my dear auntie's case, this stipulation was more flattering than the pants she wore, bringing back to my mind a statement my mom made: "Everything that says *one size fits all*, didn't take Aunt Jean into account."

"Hey, girls, you're mighty quiet. The cat's got your tongues?"

"No, they're just sitting here waiting for me to finish telling them 'bout how this fambly came to be," Grandma replied.

We all greeted Aunt Jean with warm smiles and hellos.

"Aunt Jean, do you want to join us?" I said, waving her over. "It's still a little while before the rest of the family gets here."

"Why sure, sweetie. Mama told us those stories when we were about your age. Only thing different, we were there to live part of those stories out. Always good to hear them though. Just let me get a chair from the kitchen."

Aunt Jean returned and completed the semi-circle we formed around Grandma. Anxious to start, I reminded Grandma where she had left off. "You were at the part where your Pa stormed out of the house after fussing at you and Aunt Hattie."

Grandma tilted her head to one side. "Right, right. I tell you, chil'ren, that was the start to a whole lot of trouble. It took Pa 'bout a week to say *good morning* to us—seemed more like a month though. I was right ashamed of myself, but Hattie was going on like nothing ever happened."

Grandma seemed to be lost in time, as she spoke. Her eyes had a far-away gaze. "Yeah, that Hattie had something up her sleeve, all right…something I didn't want no parts of…not at first, anyway."

Chapter 4

Grandma's Story (Plans for Escape)

I got tired of Hattie going 'round like everything was all right. She didn't seem a bit bothered by Pa being upset with us.

"What ails you, girl? Pa done fussed us out and you're going on like you own the world," I said.

She just laughed and went 'bout her way.

After a few weeks, I couldn't take her carrying on no longer. I struck up a conversation with her, 'cause something Pa said had been bothering me anyway.

"You know, Pa talked right bad 'bout Mr. Silas," I said. "I can't understand what he meant 'bout Mr. Silas buying his wife. What do you think, Hattie?"

She looked at me right dumb-like; I could tell she won't studying what I was saying. "Don't know, Bell."

I gave her the meanest look I had. "What's done got into you, girl? You're around here not paying attention and acting like you can't talk!"

Lord, what she told me could've knocked me clean off my feet.

"I's got plenty to talk about, just waiting for the right time," she replied.

"Don't be talking in no riddles. What do you got to say?"

"Well, if you want to know so bad…me and Amos is getting married."

My eyes got so wide, 'til it didn't feel like I could shut 'em. "What do you mean you're getting married?"

"Just what I said. I's getting married. But I needs your help."

"You've done lost your mind. And why are you just telling me now?"

"Cause I know'd how 'fraid you is of Pa," she said, not batting an eye. "And I had to get things in line first. Didn't need you telling nothing, 'cause if you had, I would have knocked—"

"I done had enough of your tough talk. Now this here is serious. I ain't gonna help you do nothing 'til you tell me everything."

I guess my standing up to her was a surprise. She told me all her plans.

Hattie was to leave the next Friday night, so that gave us a week to get everything ready. Amos was going to drive Buck's car 'bout half a mile from the hollow oak tree and wait there for her.

We had to figure out how to get her and her clothes out of the house, without alarming Ma and Pa. That was where I had to help.

She didn't have many clothes, so it won't too hard to fetch a box to hide 'em in. I put the box under a table by the door that had a curtain draped over it.

Hattie had a lot of smarts. She know'd just how to fool ole Pa; she went to practicing days before, without us knowing what she was up to. That girl would get up late hours and go to the outhouse. Course, when she first done it, Pa was at the door waiting for her to come back in. He questioned her 'bout it, seeing we had chamber pots in the room. She done told Pa, her stomach been bothering her and she didn't want to smell up the house, so she decided to go outdoors. Pa just nodded his head like he understood. He seemed to be right grateful that she chose to do that. She kept that up 'til all the worry left Pa.

****

Friday night came. We said our sad *good-byes*. Hattie promised to talk to me through the hollow oak tree.

"Don't worry, Bell, I'll let you know how I's making

out. I hope it won't be long before you join me. You and Buck need to do the same thing."

I couldn't find no words to answer...no nerve either...too much emotion in me to speak. Guess my eyes done said it all.

She didn't waste no time. She snuck out of the room, grabbed her box from under the table by the door, and left.

After I figured enough time went by, I eased out of the room, opened and closed the door to make it seem like she came back in.

When I got back in my bed, I pulled the covers over my head and wished I could disappear before morning.

When Pa found out Hattie was gone, he done questioned me up one side and down the other. I couldn't find enough heart to lie, so I told him she ran off to marry Amos.

Pa got his gun and went looking for them. He stayed out all day—way 'til evening. Thank God, he couldn't find 'em.

It became mighty lonely 'round there without Hattie, but she kept her promise 'bout talking through the oak. Near 'bout every letter she wrote tried to persuade me to make my escape.

It won't that easy for me, 'cause ever since she left, Ma and Pa tightened the reins on me. They watched every move I made. I couldn't go outside without Ma peeking through the curtains at me. I had to be in the house before the sun even thought about going down. When we went to church, Lena had to walk me to the outhouse. I felt just like a prisoner and I got right sick of it. More and more I thought about doing what Hattie said. I told her that, too, in one of my letters—that was all she needed.

After a little while, I got two letters in the oak tree. I thought she had a lot to say and couldn't fit it all in one envelope. Come to find out, one letter was from her and the other one from Buck, asking me to marry him. Felt like my heart stopped beating, and I broke out into a cold sweat.

Things just kept getting worse and worse 'round home. One day, I left a note in the hollow oak, accepting his offer. Me and Hattie started planning my escape.

****

Early Sunday morning, I started the first part of our plan. I put a few things I wanted to take with me in an old burlap sack. I stitched it tight—couldn't risk nothing falling out.

Ma and Pa always took something from our garden to the older sisters at church. It was my job to fill the bushel baskets in the morning. I made sure the house was quiet. I slid the sack under the same table that hid Hattie's clothes. I figured once everybody was up and busy, I could sneak it onto the cart before Pa hitched the mule. I crept back into my room and waited for Ma's call. The first part of the plan was done.

"Bell, time to get up."

It was a normal morning: Ma left to gather eggs, Lena fetched the wash water to heat on the woodstove, and Pa was out tending the hogs. I grabbed the sack from under the table and headed for the front porch. I carried it like it was real heavy—just in case somebody's eyes were spying me. I gathered a few sweet potatoes and greens in two bushel baskets. I loaded them on the cart, in front of my burlap sack. Part two of the plan was done.

Lena was the third part of my plan—she didn't know it though. She was the lead soprano on the choir, and she hated to be late.

I was real quiet on the ride to church—too quiet.

"Bell, what ails you?" Lena said.

"Don't feel the best," I said, pointing to my stomach. I didn't lie. I had a bad case of nerves. Again.

"You might feel better once we get to church. I'm leading *Blessed Assurance*."

"Uh huh," I moaned.

That's all I needed. Lena was sure gonna be in a hurry to get on the choir stand. My plan was falling into place.

When we got to church, Pa tied the mule beside the others. I made sure I took my ole sweet time getting out of the cart.

"Lena, I got to go to the outhouse."

"Now, Bell? You knows I got to get inside."

"You can go on without me."

"And have Pa skin me?" She made a sucking sound through her teeth. "Let's go, but don't take too long."

Lena waited outside, practicing her song.

I don't know who was worse, me or her. She was anxious for me to come out, and I was anxious to get out.

Hattie was good at coming up with plans. I didn't know how easy my escape was gonna be. Seemed like that girl know'd every move we were gonna make. She, Amos, and Buck were waiting a half mile down the road for me. If I ran as fast as my heart was beating, I'd be at the meeting spot long before Ma and Pa could figure out what had happened.

"How much longer are you gonna be?" Lena said, knocking on the door.

"Don't know. I may be awhile," I said, moaning.

"I's got to go," she huffed.

I could see a little more light through the cracks—I know'd she'd left.

I waited for a spell. I eased the door open and peeked out. I figured it wouldn't be long before Ma or Pa realized I won't with her. I had to act quick. I rushed to the cart to grab my sack. I tried pulling it out from behind the bushel baskets. It wouldn't move—it was caught on something. I yanked and yanked. It wouldn't budge. I had to get inside the cart.

I moved the sweet potatoes and greens out of the way. My sack was caught on a ragged piece of wood. I finally freed it. I moved the bushel baskets back in place. Then, something happened that I didn't plan.

"Hey, Bell, what you doing in that cart?"

Pa! He came out to check on me.

"F-F-Figured I'd...I'd get something...since...since I was out here."

"Gal, you know we do that after service," he said, walking closer.

I had to hide the sack. Pa was sure to know that I was up to something other than fetching baskets. I picked up the basket of greens real quick. "At least let me take 'em to the door," I said, kicking the sack next to the sweet potatoes.

"Do what I say, gal," he said. "I thought you was so sick." He stood at the cart and looked mighty worried with me. Thank goodness he was looking at me instead of inside the cart.

"Feeling some better now," I said, putting the greens basket back down in front of my sack.

"That's good. Better get on inside, so you won't miss Lena's song."

Pa helped me down. I did feel better—'bout not getting caught. My next problem was making sure I was the one who fetched them baskets after service.

****

Service ended. Pa headed outside. My stomach started bothering me for real. I wanted to run after him, but my feet wouldn't move. Pa was getting closer to the cart. He was sure to see the burlap sack. He reached the side of the cart. I closed my eyes.

"Brother Tom, let me give you a hand with that," Deacon Knight said, running over to my Pa.

My eyes popped open. Pa turned toward him when he lifted the basket of greens out of the cart. I let out a sigh of relief. Deacon Knight was a talker. He grabbed the basket of sweet potatoes and kept talking, as they walked back toward the church. They didn't seem to see the sack. That was a close one, but I still had to figure out how to hide it on the way home.

Different members were filling up the churchyard. Lena was busy talking to her choir folks and Ma was cooking in the kitchen. I slowly walked over to the cart.

"Bell, child, you're just the one I want to see." It was Mother Roundtree, a very heavy-set woman, who always called on the children to fetch things for her—saving her some steps, she'd say.

"How're you doing, Mother Roundtree?" I said.

"Better now that I've seen you. How 'bout you get

yo' daddy's bushel baskets out of my cart over yonder? He brought me the best tasting turnip greens last Sunday. Figured he could fill them baskets up again for me," she said, giving a greedy smile.

"Yes, ma'am!" I said, racing to her cart.

I used them empty baskets to hide my sack.

My ride home was sweet. The worst part of my day was over. I just had to tell Hattie and Buck what had happened—that was better than being skinned by Pa.

Chapter 5

Shocked

It was hard for me to imagine Grandma being any different from the staunch, religious figure in our lives. I never knew an adventurous, young woman hid beneath her surface. A devilish smile crept across my face—thinking on Grandma's deviance. The heat rose to my cheeks, like someone who had intruded on a personal secret. *Does anyone else feel embarrassed?*

"Grandma," Cherie gasped, "you actually tried to elope?"

"What did I tell you 'bout them fancy words, child?" Grandma said, looking confused. "Talk plain."

"You tried to run away to get married?" Cherie explained.

"Well, I was young and things were different 'long then. Don't get no ideas though, 'cause I got plenty of battle scars from not listening to my folks."

"This is so exciting," Cherie said, moving to the edge of her seat.

"I know," Pat agreed. "I didn't expect this kind of story at all."

"Every story got a beginning, a middle, and an end. But the lesson you get out of it is what makes it worth the telling," Grandma said, giving us that wise-owl look.

Grandma had thrown a thread of her life into the room, winding it around us, until we were wrapped in a tight web of togetherness—captivated by the life of Lula Bell Dupree. Coolness swept across my face, taking my embarrassment with it.

"So what happened after that?" I asked. "How did you and Pa-Pa ever end up getting—"

"Mama," Aunt Margaret yelled, as the screen door banged shut. "I brought two lemon meringue pies for tonight."

"Just put 'em in the Kelvinator," Grandma replied. "We're all sitting here in the den."

"Getting pretty tight in here," Aunt Margaret said, looking for space in the refrigerator.

She made the usual stop at the buffet, shuffled through the mail, and finally made her appearance into the den.

"What's going on in here?" she asked.

"Grandma was telling us about how she tried to run away to marry Pa-Pa," Cherie said, with a wide-eyed excitement.

"Oh my, I love to hear that story. Just let me grab a chair," Aunt Margaret said. "I hope I didn't miss my favorite part."

Aunt Margaret widened the semi-circle we formed around Grandma. "So where were you, Mama?"

"I had just finished telling them about how I almost got caught trying to run away," Grandma said. "It took me a little while to build up enough nerve to try again, but it won't long before Hattie came up with another plan—more risky than the first."

Chapter 6

Grandma's Story
(Plans for Escape II)

Ma usually made a trip to town once a month—taking me and Lena with her. I found out which Saturday she had planned to go, and I left a letter for Hattie in the oak. The next letter from her was the plan.

When we got to town, Ma and Lena saw Mrs. Bessie Robinson and her daughter, Rose, inside the store. Rose was 'bout Lena's age, and she was just like her mama: full of talk. When they spotted us, they got a hold of Ma and Lena and started gossiping.

Ma was busy laughing and asking questions. Lena and Rose talked about what fellas they were courting.

It all worked out for me—nobody paid me no attention. I acted like I was looking 'round, then I peeked at them to see if they noticed. They didn't. I made my way closer and closer to the door. Nobody looked in my direction. I eased outside and stood there awhile—just in case they'd come after me. They didn't. That seemed easy enough, but I remembered what had happened with the last plans. I walked real slow and easy to the mule cart—waiting for somebody to come calling for me. Nobody did. I went to the other side of the cart and faced the store. There was still no sign of Ma or Lena coming after me. Only one more part to the plan—run!

Like a flash of lightning had hit me, I took off down the road through town. It seemed as though wings took a hold of my feet, 'til I ran right past the spot I was supposed to meet Hattie.

"Bell, Bell, slow down!" she said, running after me.

I came to a stop when I heard her. I needed to catch my breath.

"I seen you coming," she said. "You was moving like the wind. You ready?"

"D-Don't know, Hattie," I said, gasping for air.

She grabbed my arm and pulled me in the direction of the car. When I seen Buck and Amos, my knees buckled and I didn't move no further.

"Come on, Bell, what you stopping for?" she asked, looking right disgusted.

"I'm scared, Hattie, I don't think I can do it."

"You the one living like a prisoner. If you go back, won't be no other chance," she said, releasing my arm.

I just stood there. Hattie left me and got in the car. They all sat there staring at me.

"B-e-e-e-l-l!" a distant voice called.

My joints started working again. I jumped toward the car like I had springs in my feet. Buck didn't give me a chance to change my mind; he stepped on the gas before I could sit down good—knocking me into Hattie's lap. Felt like I was riding a bucking horse; I reckoned that's how he got his name.

"Bell, sit up," she said, nudging me.

I didn't move.

"Bell...Bell...good Lord, Buck, stop the car...Buck, stop the car...please stop the car. I think Bell's done had a fit!" Hattie said, shaking me.

Buck didn't answer. He kept that ole lead foot of his to the floor. He acted like he was the one who was having a fit.

"I-I'm all right, Hattie," I answered. "I just can't sit up. B-Buck's driving too fast. First time I've ever been in a car."

"Girl, you had me mighty scared. Thought the fits done got you," Hattie said, laughing.

Buck kept driving, looking straight ahead. He won't listening to nobody.

"Slow down, Buck, your turn's coming up," Amos said.

Buck kept driving like Amos hadn't said a thing.

"What're you doing? Your turn was back there," Amos said, pointing to the road we'd just passed.

"I know," Buck said, "I ain't gonna get married there. I'm going to the courthouse in Bethel."

"Bethel?" we all said in shock.

"Yeah, I don't want y'alls daddy coming after me with no gun, like he done Amos," Buck said, keeping his eyes on the road.

****

We made our vows, with Hattie and Amos as our witnesses. Afterwards, we took them home. Then it all hit me—I was married.

I was sitting in a car by myself, with a man other than Pa. Buck was awfully quiet. That was mighty strange. I couldn't take the quiet no longer. "Sure is thirsty right about now. Can we stop to get a soda?"

Buck didn't answer. I could tell his mind was somewhere else. I asked again, just a little louder. He kept driving. I got good and fed up with him not talking to me, especially knowing how much he ran his mouth.

"Don't you hear me talking to you, Buck?"

"Just thinking, Bell, just thinking."

"Can we get a soda?" I said, a lil softer.

"Not right now."

"Why?"

He went quiet on me again.

"I said *why*."

What he told me made me sick to my stomach. "I ain't got two pennies to rub together...that's why. I had to borrow money from my older brother, Bill, just for us to get married."

"Now, Willis Steele, what in the world are you talking about? What happened to all that money you showed off at Mr. Wiley's store in front of everybody?" I had lost all my nervous feeling and looked right at him. "If you ain't got no money, then where are we gonna stay?"

"Don't know, Bell."

"What do you mean you don't know? You done got me to marry you, and you ain't got nowhere for us to stay? Don't tell me my Pa was right," I said, with hurt filling every inch of my heart.

"Don't worry, we'll be all right; I plan on staying with my folks 'til I can get us a house."

"How long's that gonna take, with you starting with nothing?" I said. "You showed off at Mr. Wiley's—pulling out big wads of money. What happened to it, anyway?"

Buck answered real slow, like every breath had to be pulled out of him. "I got something to tell you. All that money you saw…was just…just a few dollars wrapped 'round a corncob. The last one came off to get our marriage license. I ain't got enough now even for gas."

Chil'ren, I was so shocked, mad, and disappointed. Not so much with him, but with myself, for being so foolish. I never thought about how this fella was gonna take care of me.

He done fooled me into marrying him. Worst of all, I didn't have a stitch of clothes other than the ones on my back. I just sat there and let the tears cool my burning face.

****

It was evening time when we finally got to his folks' house. He told me to sit in the car while he went inside. He was gone so long, 'til I snuck out of the car and went up to the porch to find out what was holding him up.

The kitchen window was up—voices came through nice and clear. I figured I'd blend in with the dark; I peeked in.

I heard Mr. Silas' deep voice, questioning Buck. "So who's this fool gal done married you? She must not have known you ain't got nothing."

"I did the same thing you did to Mama—I used the ole corncob."

Mr. Silas throwed his head back and laughed like a monster.

"Boy, guess I done rubbed off on you. Don't know what done got into you and Amos with this running off to get married," Mr. Silas said. "I teased your Uncle Jack 'bout his new daughter-in-law. Don't know what Amos saw in that tar-baby-looking gal of Tom Dupree's. Hate to have her for a niece, but that's a problem for Jack. So who you done ran off and married?"

By this time, it looked like a knot rose in Buck's throat big enough to choke a horse. He just stood there and wouldn't say a thing.

"Don't you hear me talking to you, boy?"

Buck opened his mouth real slow and said in a mouse-like whisper, "L-L-Lula....Bell...Du-Du-Dupree."

Mr. Silas took those gigantic hands of his and grabbed Buck by his collar. He pushed Buck so hard into a chair, 'til it done toppled over. Buck's foot caught the cuff of Mr. Silas' breeches and made him fall right on top of him. Buck scrambled up and jumped backwards.

"What you looking at me fo', boy?" Mr. Silas yelled from the floor. "Help me up."

Buck pulled his Pa up real quick and jumped out of his reach.

"You 'bout the dumbest child I got. Here you call yo'self pulling my trick and you done hooked yo'self a tar-baby, too. How dare you compare yo'self to me," Mr. Silas blasted. "That gal's a far cry from being like yo' mama. I got the cream and you done got the clabber, with all them knots. Boy, you shamed me."

By this time, Mrs. Emma Steele came in. She was a pretty woman—looked almost white. But she had a sour face with deep wrinkles across her forehead.

"Silas, what's all the ruckus this time of night? Sounds like y'alls fighting in here. And what you hollering at that boy fo'?"

"Buck done fooled Tom Dupree's black daughter into marrying him. Then, had the nerve to want to bring her here to stay," Mr. Silas answered.

"Just 'til I can get us a house, Mama, that's all," Buck said. "Not that long."

"Now, Buck, what you go and do a thing like that fo'—knowing how much enemy Tom Dupree is to yo' daddy," she said, placing her hands on her hips.

"I know, Mama, but I love her and I ain't got nowhere to stay right now. Matter of fact, she's probably sitting out there wondering what's taking me so long."

"'Well, you might as well go out there and sit with her, 'cause she ain't coming in here," Mr. Silas said. "Ain't nobody as dark as me coming under this here roof to stay."

That pretty woman turned into the most evil-looking thing I'd ever seen, when Mr. Silas said that. She got in his face and pointed her bony finger right between his eyes. "Silas, you got some nerve acting this-a-way, you bald-headed rascal. Seems like you would've learnt some sense by now."

Her face turned into a tight point, with her neck stretched forth like a turtle's. "As black as you is, you acting like something you ain't. You done enough damage to that boy already, ain't no need to do no mo'. If you send him away, who's gonna run your store?"

She moved real close to Mr. Silas until their lips almost touched. "If you know what's bess for you, Silas Steele, you better swallow that ole color-struck pride of yours. If Buck can't stay here, then you can't either."

Mr. Silas dropped his head like a defeated dog.

Ms. Emma turned to Buck, lifting her chin high in the air. "Make sure you let that gal know that there's only *one* Mrs. Steele 'round here—Emma Faye Davis Steele. Go clean out the spare bedroom in the back, then get that gal you call yo' wife."

When they all left the kitchen, I dragged myself back to the car. My heart felt like it had weights on it—if only I had listened to Pa.

****

Later that evening, I felt like I was gonna burst if I didn't say something to Buck about what I'd heard. "Buck, I got something to tell you," I whispered. "I know I shouldn't have, but I got out of the car when you took so long coming back. I heard almost everything your folks said about me."

"Bell, I'm sorry you had to hear all that," he said, looking right pitiful. "Daddy's set in his ways. And

Mama…she's been bitter after what happened to our family."

Buck looked afar off, like he was talking to somebody else. "Seems like he'd remember what he'd done. But I guess ain't no changing him. He didn't do right by us either, especially Ethel." His voice trembled a bit and cracked. He cleared his throat. "That's enough talking, Bell."

He went quiet on me. Again. The next thing I heard was his snoring. My mind was spinning. *Who is Ethel? And what have I gotten myself into?* I had jumped from the frying pan straightway into the fire—I cried myself to sleep.

Chapter 7

Dinner Time

"Speaking of frying pan, I'd better get in that kitchen and start frying them fish," Grandma said. "The rest of the fambly's gonna be here soon and I wants to make sure them fish is ready by six o'clock."

Grandma scrambled into the kitchen; pots and pans clanged, while cabinet doors squeaked opened and slammed shut.

Grandma normally fasted on Fridays, so eating at six o'clock was of utmost importance.

The other family members filtered in. We couldn't help but tell them about all we had heard. I was completely awestruck; I believe Cherie and Pat were, too.

Grandma's house became lively with conversations breaking out in the kitchen, dining room, and den, while the sizzling and popping sounds of frying fish set the mood for feasting.

I was cradled in the unity of my family, as I gazed from aunt to uncle, to cousin, to mom, to dad, to Grandma.

As the time drew closer to six o'clock, we started preparing the dining room for dinner. I helped Aunt Margaret set the table, while Cherie and Pat fixed the plates. Grandma set big pitchers of lemonade on each end of the table, while Aunt Jean brought little baskets of cornbread out.

Uncle Leroy retold his fishing stories—reliving how each fish ended up in the pan.

The little ones giggled about splashing water at the

bathroom sink, while Aunt Nettie scolded.

It was a normal gathering, yet it seemed unfamiliar. *How did we become such a close-knit family, especially if we hadn't always been that way? Grandma would have to complete her story for me to understand.*

"Renee, what're you doing standing over there in the corner? Come sit down so we can bless the food, child," Grandma said, breaking into my unconscious state of mind.

I didn't realize everybody was seated and waiting for me. Uncle Mason blessed the table and we all started eating, enjoying the family time, while the fishbone piles grew higher and higher.

"Mama, since we got all the family sitting around the table, you ought to finish telling the girls about your life with grandpa and grandma Steele," Aunt Jean suggested.

"I guess this is about as good a time as any," Grandma said, looking more refreshed, after breaking her fast.

"I was talking to the girls 'bout our hist'ry and how I married their Pa-Pa," Grandma explained to the rest of the family. "I believe I was at the part when we got to his folks' house."

I nodded to confirm her statement.

"The first few months of married life won't nothing like I expected," Grandma said. "It reminded me of that story you read to your baby cousins, Renee. You know the one 'bout that girl with the mean sisters and mama. They just made her do all the work and treated her like a dog."

"Oh, you mean *Cinderella*," I said, picking up on Grandma's one-of-a-kind description.

"Yeah, that's it, child, Rella. That's just who I felt like, that girl Rella, except I didn't have no prince to take me nowheres. Matter of fact, we couldn't go nowheres for a long time—just had to stay there with them contrary folks of his."

Little snickers skipped from one end of the table to the other, until it hit Grandma. "Thinking 'bout it, tickles me now," she started, "but believe me, 'long then I didn't have much laugh in me."

Chapter 8

Grandma's Story
(The Morning After)

When I woke up Sunday morning, I didn't know where I was, what day it was, or the time. I jolted up in the bed and looked around—trying to figure out my whereabouts.

I know'd I won't home, 'cause the house was more fancy than ours. The room had pretty, flower-print curtains at the windows, nice furniture, and a fancy washbowl and pitcher in the corner. The bed was real soft, not like the corn shucks I'd slept on 'bout all my life. I guess that's why I'd slept so long.

Then it all hit me—I was married. I sat there all alone. I felt right frightful being in Buck's folks' house with no kin 'round me. The only one I thought would protect me was him, and he'd left me. I got to feeling right sorry for myself all over again, 'til the tears took a hold of me.

My crying was cut short when I heard a strange sound coming through the wall. I got real quiet. It was a man's voice, but it won't Mr. Silas' nor Buck's. I eased my way out of the bed, walked softly to the door, and pressed my ear hard against it. I had to strain my ears, but I realized it was a preacher, preaching right in Mr. Silas' house. I thought, *my God, these folks even buy preachers.*

I couldn't understand why nobody woke me. I didn't bother going out. My mind got on my folks and how they were probably at Mt. Holly 'round 'bout that time. I know'd it would be a long time before I could face Ma and Pa, especially after what I'd done. My eyes filled up again.

After 'while, a loud static noise startled me—

everything went quiet. That's when I realized that preacher was coming across a radio.

Course my folks didn't have one, but Mr. Wiley did, that's how I know'd what the sound was. I figured whatever was going on, was probably over—I didn't know what to do. I reckoned somebody would be calling for me soon. I couldn't greet nobody with my face all messy, but I was afraid to leave the room to pump myself some water.

I went over to the fancy washbowl in the corner. It was sitting in a pretty stand, made of fine cherry wood. The pitcher was underneath on a little shelf. Something told me to pick it up. When I did, bless my God, it had water in it already. I reckoned Buck had left it there for me. I could've kissed him for that. I washed my face and hurried to get dressed.

Not long afterwards, Buck came into the room with some breakfast for me.

"Morning, Bell, how'd you rest?"

"Too good, I guess. I didn't even hear you leave me this morning. It kind of bothered me to see you were gone. You know I'm your new bride."

"Didn't mean to worry you, baby doll," he said, setting my plate on the dresser. "I usually listen to the radio with my Daddy on Sunday mornings—didn't want to disturb you."

"Speaking of radio, who was that preacher y'all were listening to?"

"That was Bishop S.C. Johnson. We never heard nobody preach like him, and he's 'bout the only man Daddy can't find no fault with, yet."

"I ain't never heard of him."

"He's out of Philadelphia, but he's got churches down here, too. Maybe—"

"Buck! Come on and eat yo' breakfast," Ms. Emma yelled. Her high-pitched voice sent chills down my spine.

Buck rushed out, leaving me there to eat my breakfast alone. I didn't have much of an appetite—just picked at my food. It swelled up in my mouth when I tried to swallow it.

My mind was twirling with all kinds of thoughts

and I couldn't settle on not one of 'em. I won't sure what I needed to do, as far as coming out of the room. I was afraid to sit there and afraid to leave.

After 'while, Buck came back. "Bell, you hardly touched your food," he said, sitting down next to me. "You feeling all right?"

"No, I ain't feeling good at all," I said, pinching my lips tight, to keep them from quivering.

He got down on his knees in front of me, and studied my face. "What's troubling you?"

My eyes started stinging and my throat tightened. "I don't belong here."

"You belong with me, whether it be here or wherever," he said, stroking my face. "You're my wife now."

"Wife or no wife, your folks despise me."

By that time, I'd done given myself over to crying and trembling. The plate was jumping so hard in my hands, 'til Buck took it from me and sat it on the floor. He held my hands in a firm grip to steady me. He let me have my cry, 'til it seemed like I didn't have no more tears left. Then he pulled out a handkerchief and gently wiped my face.

"Bell, you stay in the room for the rest of the day. I'll tell my folks you don't feel well."

He left, taking my plate of half-eaten food with him. I spent the rest of that day hiding and crying.

Buck had to spend part of the day setting up the store for Monday. I was glad when he finally joined me that evening. I figured I'd feel better having him in the room with me, but I couldn't get no peace that night, 'cause the walls of that house were mighty thin. I could hear Mr. Silas and Ms. Emma talking through them—'bout me.

I don't think Buck heard them, 'cause as soon as his head hit the pillow, he was asleep—like a rock. He needed his rest, 'cause he had to open the store early the next day. His slow, heavy breathing didn't block out what I heard though.

"Emma, I don't want that gal cooking nothing fo' me," Mr. Silas said. "I hate to think about them black hands touching my food. Just have her chop wood for the stove, or whatever else you need done 'round here."

"Silas, I'm 'bout sick and tired of you and yo' color talk. Don't know what'll take to get through that thick skull of yours," Ms. Emma said. "And you don't have to tell me how to run my house. I ain't 'bout to let no half-raised gal come in here and take over."

"I-I didn't mean no harm, Emma. Just that I knows her fambly—she ain't come from the same stock as us. They's a lot lower."

"Of course they is, and 'bout lazy as they come— laying 'round all day. She might have fooled Buck, but I knows her kind," Ms. Emma said.

"Let her work with that *cloth*. That ought to break her in," Mr. Silas said. "I hate for anybody to know she's connected to this fambly. And for God's sake, don't ever let her go to the store with Buck. If you run out of things fo' her to do, send her to the tobacco fiel' with the hired help."

"That's 'bout where she belongs," Ms. Emma said. "I knows just what to do with her. Now shut yo' mouth so I's can rest."

Chapter 9

Understanding Great-Grandpa Steele

"Grandma, that doesn't make any sense," Pat said, looking like she was about to explode. "If great-grandpa Steele was as dark as you, why was he so hard against you?"

Talking about spinning heads around like hoot owls, Grandma seemed awfully startled with Pat's sudden outburst. After regaining her composure, she settled herself backwards into the arms of her chair.

"Let me tell you something, baby. When people try to be something they ain't, the first thing they do is deny who they are," Grandma said. "When something comes 'round to remind them, they try their best to kill it—get it out of the way quick, so they won't have to face the truth. But, when you're *real* on the inside, you won't mind what you *look* like on the outside."

Pat nodded, as if she was absorbing the knowledge released upon all of us.

What did Cherie think of that?

"Now, in addition to that, I didn't let his hatred toward me cause me to be spiteful against him. I know'd that wouldn't mend things. *Two wrongs* surely don't make things right," Grandma concluded.

Now, that was a nice punch for Pat. Did she get the message?

Pat and Cherie shifted in their seats. I wasn't sure what they were thinking, but the heat of Grandma's words was enough to make my ears hot. The dining room transformed into a courtroom: Grandma was the judge, the rest of the family were the jurors, and I was the witness, who was afraid to speak. *Would anybody break the spell...please?*

Aunt Margaret poured herself another glass of lemonade. The *tinkling* ice, moving around in the pitcher, finally resumed things.

"Mama, you've been talking for quite a bit, would you care for something to drink?"

"I guess I will, Margaret," Grandma replied, passing her glass down the table.

My eyes focused on Grandma's glass. The greasy fingerprints smeared together, as each person grabbed it and passed it to Aunt Margaret. My ears cooled, as I watched the ice dance around and float to the top of Grandma's full glass of lemonade—I was refreshed.

"Well, getting back to what I was saying," Grandma continued, "I heard 'bout all of Mr. Silas and Ms. Emma's talk, through them walls. I guess it was a good thing though, at least I know'd what I was in store for."

Chapter 10

Grandma's Story (Misery)

I was resting good that Monday morning—it didn't last long.

BANG, BANG, BANG. "Bell Dupree, get yo' lazy self up, gal. We ain't gonna have you laying 'round here all day."

Ms. Emma was a little woman, but she sounded like she was gonna tear my bedroom door down.

I jumped up like the house was on fire and opened the door. "Yes, ma'am, I'm up."

"Gal, if you ain't one sight, I do declare. Wash yo' filthy face—got sleep all 'round yo' mouth."

"Yes, ma'am," I said, feeling right ashamed. If there was a hole in the floor, I would've crawled in it.

"Hurry up and get dressed, so I can tell you some rules 'round here," Ms. Emma said, storming away with her skirt tail switching 'round them scrawny legs of hers.

I washed my face real good, twice, dressed and hurried into the kitchen. Ms. Emma laid right into me. "We's a business fambly. Being that you ain't got that kind of mind, your job is to work 'round the house. I hope you got some learning 'bout that."

"Yes, ma'am, I do."

She started me with chopping wood. From there, I had to sweep the yard, just in case company came. I dusted furniture and cleaned the house. But the thing that stuck in my mind the most was how I had to scrub the floors on my hands and knees, with a tiny cloth—not much bigger than my hand.

"Yo' mama probably don't have no nice floors like these. So I's got to teach you how to take care of things," Ms. Emma said, dangling the cloth in my face.

"Yes, ma'am."

"And don't take all day either, there's plenty of work to be done 'round here."

I didn't know how in the world she expected me not to take all day, especially when I had to keep unballing the cloth after every few strokes. By the time I finished, I could hardly stand up straight.

"Why you walking like that fo', gal?" she said, smirking.

"My back's bothering me a little, ma'am," I answered.

"You ain't got no back, just a gristle."

I tried to stand tall, but my back was hurting so bad, 'til it felt like it was gonna break.

I remembered what Mr. Silas had told Ms. Emma 'bout sending me to the fields, if she couldn't find nothing for me to do. I figured I'd never see them fields.

****

By early evening, I was plumb worn out. I sat on the front porch, waiting for Buck to get home from the store. It seemed like I got more refreshed when I seen him drive up the path. There was somebody else in the car with him; I straightened myself up a bit, to keep from looking throwed away.

"How're you doing, baby doll," Buck said, coming up the porch steps.

"Coming 'long," I replied, standing to greet him.

"This is my oldest brother, Bill. He helps me at the store sometimes."

"Pleasure to meet you," I said.

"Same here," he replied, smiling.

"I told Bell how you helped me get the marriage license," Buck said.

"He sure did," I started, "thank you for that."

"No problem," Bill said. "I see it was well worth it."

I felt the heat rise to my face; I dropped my eyes. He had the same flatter talk Buck did—caught me by surprise, but it was better than the way his folks talked to me.

"I told Bill it was 'bout time he settled down," Buck said, nudging Bill on the shoulder.

"You ain't married, yet?" I asked.

"I'm working on it," Bill said, smiling again. "I've been keeping company with a girl from Ahoskie. I might bring her 'round to meet Mama and Daddy sooner or later."

"At least you got a house of your own to put her in," Buck said, laughing. "So they can't say too much."

"I reckon you're right about that," Bill said. "Well, don't keep your bride standing out here, Buck, it's supper time."

Buck put his arm 'round me, as we walked into the house. Mr. Silas was already seated and his mama had set the plates on the table—four.

"Is there something I can do to help you, Ms. Emma?" I asked.

"Naw," she said, without looking at me. "Boys, get washed up, yo' daddy's ready to eat.

Buck and Bill headed to the pump on the back porch. I followed.

When we went back into the kitchen, we all stood around. I guess Buck and Bill were waiting for me to sit first. I won't sure which seat was mine and I didn't want to take no chances.

"Where do you want me to sit, Ms. Emma?"

"Ain't no room for you at the table," Mr. Silas said. "You gonna have to eat out back."

Bill's face turned into a scowl. "Daddy, now that ain't—"

"Hush yo' mouth, Bill, this don't concern you," Mr. Silas said, giving him a threatening look.

"Then I'll eat at home," Bill replied, storming out the door.

"That won't change nothing," Mr. Silas yelled after

him.

"Then I'll eat out back with Bell," Buck said, grabbing his plate and the one Bill had left. "You and Mama can have the kitchen all to yourself."

Me and Buck ate in silence.

Chapter 11

Loss of Appetite

A family is where you're supposed to be nourished and grow, isn't it? How did Grandma become the beautiful person she was, with such strong roots? Especially with little sunshine and all rain.

"Speaking of eating, Renee, you ain't hardly touched your food, child," Grandma said, pinching the tender flesh from the other side of her fish.

Little piles of bones sat beside everyone's plate, except mine. The sadness of Grandma's story filled the spot in my stomach where my food should have been. "It's hard to eat when I hear the things you went through."

"I know how you feel, baby, but that was a long time ago," Grandma said in a loving tone. "I didn't have much appetite them days either. I made up for it since then though."

We all laughed. Grandma had the highest pile of bones.

Cherie put another fish on my plate and Pat sat the basket of cornbread in front of me. I had no choice. Hearty eating was a family tradition. I nibbled my cornbread and pinched my fish. It was forced eating, but delicious.

Grandma seemed to be overjoyed with watching us all eat. I was starting to understand why it was so important to her for us to sit around the table together. Our Friday night meals would never be the same again—not just a gathering, a union.

"You must have thought about your family a lot," I

said, pinching at another piece of fish.

"Nearly every minute of the day," Grandma said. "Pa said Mr. Silas was as evil as a snake. I started to see some of what he meant. One thing he forgot was that hornet-sting wife of his. I wished I had listened to Pa."

"Great-grandpa and grandma Steele didn't try to do anything to make you feel welcomed?" Pat asked.

"I wasn't welcomed. They made that clear from the start," Grandma said. "It was one of those situations that would either make you or break you. I might have been bent, but they couldn't break me."

Chapter 12

Grandma's Story (Tobacco Fields)

My days 'round there didn't get no better. My knees ached from cleaning them floors at least twice a day. Ms. Emma always found some excuse to go out to the pigpen, and then leave a trail of mud on my clean floors. One good thing happened though, that tiny cloth finally wore out. Bless my God, I was able to use a regular rag.

I never know'd what she went outside for, 'cause I was the one who tended everything: cleaned the coop, gathered the eggs, milked the cow, slopped the hogs, and took care of their stubborn goats. As if that wasn't enough, as soon as it was time to prime the tobacco, I made my way to them fields.

The field hands won't too friendly at first. I reckoned they thought Mr. Silas had sent me out there to spy—those who even knew I was his daughter-in-law.

"What you doing out here, gal?" A big, round woman asked me on my first day in the field. Later, I found out her name was Thelma.

"Mr. Silas sent me out here to help," I whispered.

"Ain't you the one who married one of his sons?"

"Yes, ma'am, I married Buck."

"I told Mary you won't no hired help. She declared you was, 'specially the way we seen you working 'round there."

My eyes stung and my top lip quivered.

"Now, now, child, ain't no need to look like that," Thelma said. "I can tell you ain't know'd much 'bout that family. If you had, you would've never married Buck."

"My Pa told me some things," I said, choking back the tears.

"Well, he must not have told you the *right* things. But ain't no need crying over spilled milk. You's in the family now. I reckon you gots to earn your keep."

I nodded.

"What's your name, child?"

"Bell."

"How much you know 'bout 'bacca, baby?" she asked, giving my shoulder a tight squeeze.

"Not much," I said, feeling the pressure leave my heart. Thelma reminded me of my own Ma. I could tell by the look in her eyes, she know'd 'bout how I was feeling.

"Don't you worry, Bell, we's gonna be your field family. Stick with me and I'll teach you what you need to know."

"Thank you, ma'am," I said, smiling.

"And stop calling me, ma'am. My name's Thelma, you hear?"

"Yes, ma'am, Ms. Thelma."

She gave a quick laugh and hugged me close to her yellow, tobacco-stained dress. "I know, baby, that's the way yo' mama raised you."

Ms. Thelma introduced me to the rest of the field hands. After a few days or so of whispering and stealing glances at me, everybody seemed to trust me. They made me feel right at home—if you can call a tobacco field home.

Putting in tobacco was hard, hot work. The men did the priming: pulling the leaves off the tobacco stalk. After that, the tobacco was sent to the barn for stringing and hanging. That was my job.

At first, I handed the leaves to the stringer. I watched for weeks how they tied the tobacco leaves along a four foot long pine stick. A string was fastened to one end. They stacked about three or four leaves on one side of the stick, wrapped the string around it, and stacked three more leaves on the other side of the stick. They kept switching sides, 'til the whole stick was covered with golden leaves.

Once my time came, it took me awhile to keep the leaves from falling off, but with Ms. Thelma's help, I had some of the prettiest tied tobacco in the barn.

Between all the house work, field work, and Ms. Emma's food, my dresses started sagging. I looked right pitiful to my own self.

My scrawniness didn't get me no pity from Ms. Emma though. It seemed like she got a joy out of making me miserable. Misery won't the only thing in her heart; jealousy found a home there, too.

I remember how pitiful her garden was—it looked right snaggletooth. Course that was added to my list of chores. It took a good little while to bring it up to par.

I planted collards, kale, butter beans, green peppers, and tomatoes. I straightened the rows with broken sticks and twine. I was mighty proud of that little garden. I looked forward to talking to my plants. It seemed like they enjoyed my company, too. I'd sing to them while I pulled weeds and patted the dirt back tight—like a mother tucking in a baby. Seeing what came forth from my hands brought a little sunshine.

I hardly let anything distract me when I was busy in the garden. That is 'til one of the loud neighbors, Ms. Bertie, came by.

"My, my, you's doing a mighty fine job in that garden," she said.

"Thank you, ma'am," I said, wiping my brow with an old rag.

"I ain't never seen it look that good all the years I's been living 'round here," she said, chuckling.

I returned a smile.

"Yeah, this patch of ground was the most pitiful looking—"

"Bertie, you got business here?" Ms. Emma yelled from the porch, giving one of her bitter-turtle looks.

Ms. Bertie's countenance changed real quick. "Naw, just passing by," she said, winking at me. She went on her way.

The strangest thing happened after that. It had rained something terrible—two days in a row. When I was finally able to get to the garden, I noticed a lot of vegetables were uprooted and smashed. I know'd rain could beat a garden down and make it sloppy. But that was the first time I'd ever seen plants clean plucked out of the ground, roots and all, and throwed in other rows.

It didn't take me long to give a name to that hurricane that had come through there: Ms. Emma.

I never know'd a person could be so spiteful. Sadly enough, it was a disease that filtered from one to the other.

One day, I was looking out of the kitchen window and saw Mr. Silas easing his way over to the goats' pen. He tiptoed a few steps, looked around real sneaky-like, and tiptoed some more. I should've know'd he was up to something, but he looked so funny, 'til I took a fancy to watching him.

He unlocked the gate and ran the goats clean out of the pen. He circled 'round the barn and left. I thought that sure was a crazy thing to do, especially the way them demons chewed up everything. I reckoned he had a reason for doing it—I won't about to question him.

That afternoon, he came storming in, right up to me. "Bell, them goats is out there running loose. Gate wide open. You needs to take better care in doing yo' work 'round here."

I was so shocked, 'til I looked him dead in his eyes. He looked like he had seen a ghost. He jerked his eyes away from me.

"W-W-We didn't have these kind of problems, 'til you came 'round," he said, backing away.

"Yes, sir," I whispered, trying not to cry.

"You bess get yo'self out there and find every last one, and make sure you lock that gate," he said, rushing out of the room.

I had a time, dragging them goats back to the pen— got butted a plenty—even lost a piece of my apron to them chewing demons.

****

I tossed and turned in bed that night—my nerves wouldn't let me rest. Buck slept right peaceful, breathing with little wheezing sounds rising and falling. It would've calmed me just listening to him, but my ears caught more.

Low murmurs, evil murmurs, came through the tiny cracks of the wall. I strained to hear. Another *Bell* conversation.

"Emma, something's mighty familiar 'bout that gal's eyes. I never noticed 'em too much 'til I got on her 'bout the goats...I can't stand to look at 'em," Mr. Silas said.

"I noticed 'em, too," Ms. Emma replied.

"Right haunting, ain't they? Feels like a haint done come back."

"Something ought to haunt you, for all you done," she said.

"Oh, Emma, ain't you ever gonna forgive me?"

"I ain't the one to do the forgiving. You gots a price to pay."

"Well, yo' debt 'bout as big as mine. You ain't been no saint either," Mr. Silas grumbled.

Everything went silent.

Chapter 13

After Dinner

Everybody sat around the table, looking completely stuffed to full satisfaction. Nobody wanted another bite.

Cherie and Pat left the table to start cleaning the dishes. It was my job to clear the table, while the adults shifted, grunted, and belched before telling Grandma how good everything was.

After I cleared the last plate, Cherie returned to the dining room with a hot, soapy cloth. She wiped away the evidence of our Friday night feast—except one spot.

She had started putting the leftovers away when she heard Grandma's call: "You missed a spot, baby."

"I'll get it," Pat said, dipping the cloth up and down in the water until all the crumbs disappeared from it.

"Thanks," Cherie said softly.

"No problem," Pat replied.

Their simple conversing made a warm feeling come over me; I smiled.

Pat *sanctified* the table to Grandma's satisfaction.

Aunt Jean then placed the pineapple cake in the middle of it and two lemon meringue pies at each end. Of course, nobody had room for anything else. Grandma suggested that everybody go into the den and sit around the fire that Uncle Henry had started. Huffs and blows filled the air, as the family pushed themselves away from the table and wobbled into the den.

Cherie, Pat, and I worked in the kitchen until it was spotless. We joined the rest of the family in the den.

Everything was nice and cozy, just right for a nap, but Grandma's story had my mind on edge, and I couldn't rest until it was completed.

After gathering chairs from the kitchen and dining room, we found our spots, leaving the floor open to Grandma. She sat comfortably in her old rocker, folding her hands in the creases of her apron that carried the aroma of fried fish and hot sauce.

She slowly rocked back and forth. Her mind seemed to have been focused on a distant time. "I had some right cloudy days, chil'ren, but after 'while, the sun did shine in its time."

Chapter 14

Grandma's Story (Ray of Hope)

I got up extra early and waited for Ms. Emma in the kitchen, as usual. I had the woodstove going, but I still felt cold—chills from that *haint* talk the night before.

Don't know why in the world I strained to listen, knowing how scary I was. Whatever was haunting Mr. Silas was working on me, too. I should've waited to leave my room once I heard Ms. Emma stirring about, but for God's sake, I didn't want her to catch me with my face dirty—not again.

"Bell, what you waiting 'round fo'? Go fetch me some water, so I's can get started with breakfast," she said, coming in. "And when you finish with that, I needs you to fetch me some mo' eggs."

"Yes, ma'am."

Every morning was the same ole thing: fussing and fetching. I looked forward to seeing Buck all fresh looking and dressed businesslike before he went to tend the store. But whenever I finished one chore, Ms. Emma had me do another one. I'd only get to peek at him and Mr. Silas while they ate their breakfast.

I waited for Buck by the car, hoping he'd come out before Mr. Silas.

"I wish I could've joined you for breakfast," I said, when he finally came.

Buck looked like a child stealing candy. "I know, baby doll, things'll get better."

He gave me a quick kiss and slid into the car. I

watched him pull away down that dusty path. So many thoughts crossed my mind, but the one that stuck out the most was: *Why in the world would he bring me into a fambly like this?*

Somehow I managed to get through the day. I felt like a walking stone. Me and Buck ate our dinner on the back porch, as usual. The lump I carried in my throat made me pick at my food.

"Something bothering you, baby doll?"

Tears popped out of me like corn kernels on a hot griddle. "Buck, if you know'd how your Pa felt about dark folks, why did you marry me? I ain't felt no closeness 'round here yet...ain't seen none of the other fambly members, besides your oldest brother, Bill...and got to eat separate like some kind of dog or something."

My crying sounded more like moaning, but I kept on with my complaining. "I don't want to be here like this...I don't belong...I need something to lift my spirits...you ain't hardly here...I miss my fambly."

Mentioning my fambly brought church to my mind. "I-I want to go to my church and be with my own kind of people."

Buck wrapped his arms 'round me and tried to hush me the best he could. "Bell, I'm sorry about you feeling like this. I promise I'll try to fix things for you 'round here, and if you want to go to church, I'll take you. Just bear with me a little longer. I might have us a place real soon."

Hearing that, sent a tingling inside—a flutter of joy.

"I've been talking to this man Daddy knows, Mr. Robert Lee Jones. He has a place just up the road a piece," Buck said. "The folks he got renting it ain't doing right, so he's planning to get rid of 'em. Once they move out, we can buy the place if we want it."

My heart felt a little lighter, knowing we'd be getting our own place.

"We've got to fix it up a bit, but it's mighty nice," Buck continued. "It's got an indoor toilet and running water, too. I wanted to surprise you, but I hope this makes you feel a little better."

Before I know'd anything, I had throwed my arms

'round his neck so fast, 'til he almost fell backwards.

****

Buck took a long time coming in the room that night. I laid there listening, like I often did at times. My ears caught something new: Buck's voice. It was another *Bell* conversation.

"Daddy, I've come in here to ask one thing of you. I'm a grown man now, and I've been faithful by you and Mama. Whether you like it or not, Bell is my wife and I want her to eat with me at the table."

I heard a long silence. All I could imagine was Mr. Silas rolling his sleeves back and balling up those huge hands of his—getting ready to knock Buck out.

Ms. Emma's squeaky voice broke the silence. "Silas, you done destroyed part of that boy. You owe him that much. And you better do it if you know what's bess fo' you."

I didn't hear Mr. Silas say one word. The next sound was heavy footsteps coming to my room. I closed my eyes like I was asleep.

The next morning, Buck's mama had a place for me at the table. Now, that was a real task—to eat without making faces over the food. But at least I was able to sit next to Buck. I did have one problem though: I faced Mr. Silas.

At my folks' house, Pa always sat at the head of the table. It wasn't so in the Steele's home—Ms. Emma did. It was hard for me to eat with my head down the whole time. I looked up. My eyes met Mr. Silas'. He jerked his head so hard, 'til I wondered how his food made it down his throat. I figured he couldn't stand the looks of me. Our meals were mighty quiet.

After I joined the fambly at the table, Bill started eating dinner there again. He and Buck were a lot alike—didn't seem to care for their folks' ways. Buck did all he could to make things better 'round there for me. It didn't make much difference, 'cause Ms Emma kept me in the place she thought I belonged.

One day, there was a knock on the door. Ms. Emma was in the back, so I answered it.

"Hello, ma'am, I'm Robert Lee Jones. I'm here to see Buck, is he home?"

I answered, using the best voice I could, "No sir, but I'm his wife. Do you want me to—"

"Wife? What kind of wife is you? I'm the woman of this here house," Ms. Emma said, coming into the kitchen. "Go find some work to do."

I felt the heat rise to my face. If it was possible, I would've melted right there. I left the room as fast as I could.

I never could figure out how to prepare myself for the things I had to face every day. I passed the nights remembering how me and Hattie used to laugh and talk. I thought about how she had the courage I didn't—the courage I needed to take me through each day.

I hadn't heard from her in awhile, and I started missing my fambly more and more. I did write them right after I was married, so they wouldn't think I was shacking. They never wrote back. I longed to see them. I felt empty, especially with the strange way I spent my Sundays. I just kept on like that for months.

It was hard to talk to Buck about how I felt. He was working so hard at the store, trying to get enough money for Mr. Jones' place. Sometimes he wouldn't get in 'til late and he never noticed how I was treated.

One night, I couldn't hold it no longer. "Buck, I know you've been trying to make things better for me 'round here and all, but I needs to get out...to be 'round people who show some feeling."

"What're you talking 'bout?"

"I want to go to my church. And I don't want to wait no longer. I want to go this Sunday coming."

Buck stood there looking at me with pitiful eyes. "Will do. I'll even ask Amos and Hattie to join us. How 'bout that?"

That sent my heart to racing.

****

Sunday didn't come fast enough. I was all excited, and then the phone rang.

"Yeah, Amos, we're ready," Buck said. "Really? She's feeling that bad, huh? I'll tell Bell...all right, bye."

My heart sank.

"Bell, as you know, Hattie's in the same situation as you. She ain't feeling the best today. Amos said maybe we can get together next weekend."

It took all I had not to burst into tears. I understood Hattie's problem though. We both were expecting our first-borns.

"I kind of had my heart set on seeing my folks. I figured if we all went together, it wouldn't be no ornery stuff from Ma and Pa."

Buck nodded. "Maybe we can see them once the baby's born," he said. "You know how folks act over their grandbabies, especially their first ones."

"I guess there won't be no church for me today," I said, almost pouting.

"We can go to see the preacher Daddy listens to every Sunday. So happens he's down this way. Matter of fact, he ought to be here for a few weeks."

I had my drawbacks at first, but it was better than sitting 'round the house like I had been doing for months. Off to Bishop S. C. Johnson's church we went.

As soon as we got there, I heard low mumbling noises and I didn't see nobody but two ushers standing at the door.

"Where's everybody at?" I whispered to Buck. "And what in the world is that noise? This here's a strange kind of church."

"Quiet, Bell," Buck whispered, putting his finger to his lips. "Folks is praying."

"Where?"

He pointed between the pews at the people on their knees. Course we did things a whole lot different at Mt. Holly. Most times, we just whooped and hollered.

The ushers led me and Buck to a seat in the back of the church. We sat there for the longest time. It seemed like them folks won't never gonna get out of prayer—stayed down for a half hour or more. That was a long time. I was used to praying for 'bout ten minutes.

Somebody started singing, and the people got up and took their seats. I looked 'round and could hardly believe my eyes. I couldn't understand how Mr. Silas, being as proud as he was, even thought to listen to that preacher. At least I wore earbobs and lipstick. Them folks were as plain as they come.

I studied one woman—looked at her from head to toe. She wore a small black hat, with nothing on it: no veil or nothing. Her hair was natural, no straightening or curls, just held by a hair net. No makeup or jewelry of any kind, except a watch. She was buttoned up to the neck in a long sleeve, white blouse, starched and creased to a tee. Her long, black skirt hung near 'bout to her ankles, but I was able to see some funny kind of stockings on her legs. I found out later they were cotton stockings. And them shoes she wore were polished so shiny, 'til it look like you could almost see yourself in 'em.

She sat real humble-like, holding a Bible in her lap. Won't nothing fancy 'bout her, yet she looked mighty dignified.

A brother read a scripture, and then they started their singing and testimonies—it touched me to my very soul. I had a warm, homey feeling inside.

After 'while, I noticed everybody stood up and started singing this song called *Remember Me*. I looked in the direction everybody was staring. There he was, Bishop S. C. Johnson himself. He walked so erect down the middle of the aisle.

My eyes followed him 'til he stepped onto the pulpit. All of a sudden, he disappeared.

"Goodness gracious, Buck, where'd he go?" I said, standing on my tiptoes. "Did he fall out or something?"

I know'd about some of those healer folks, who knocked people on the forehead 'til they fell out, but I ain't never know'd the preacher to fall out, too. Had me scared there for a moment. I didn't realize I had raised my voice.

"Shhhh," Buck said, giving me a cock-eyed frown. "He gets in prayer first."

I'd seen some of the members turn around and smile at me. I guess they know'd I was a visitor. I managed to smile back before dropping my shamed head.

I figured the best thing for me to do was to try to keep my mouth shut. I did all right 'til Bishop Johnson started preaching things I'd never heard before.

"You must be born of the water and the spirit before you can enter into God's kingdom," he said.

Now, I know'd at Mt. Holly we just raised our hands and bowed our heads. Never even thought about no water. I had to check up on what he was talking 'bout.

"Buck, hand me that Bible over there," I whispered, pointing to the back of the pew in front of us.

He passed me the Bible without breaking his eyes away from the pulpit.

"What scripture did he say?" I asked, flipping through the Bible.

"Acts 2:38," Buck whispered, "and be quiet."

I drowned everything out as I turned past Matthew, Mark, Luke, John, 'til I finally hit Acts. I could hardly believe what I read. It jumped out at me like a jack-in-the-box. As much churchgoing as I had done, I'd never heard or seen that scripture before. I read it over and over again. After that, I opened my ears to all that preacher had to say.

At the end of the sermon, Bishop Johnson asked if anyone wanted to be baptized. Before I know'd anything, I sprung to my feet and raised my hand.

"What're you doing, Bell?" Buck whispered, looking right wide-eyed.

"I'm getting baptized, didn't you?"

"No, not yet."

"Hush your mouth. You mean to tell me you've been 'round this good thing and you ain't got baptized yet?"

Before he could answer, the ushers came to lead me to the dressing room. The sisters dressed me in a long, white robe, starched stiff—the purest white, I'd ever seen. They gave me a white bonnet to place on my head.

The same sister I had studied was the one who led me to the pool. A brother was already in the water waiting for me.

My stomach had a quick twitching to it; a mixture of nerves and excitement took a hold of me. The brother grabbed my hand as I stepped into the pool—that settled my stomach and gave me confidence. The water was so cold, 'til it sent chills up my legs. I waded through it to the middle. The chill rose up to my waist, but I felt warm inside.

The people gathered 'round and sang, *Going Down in Jesus Name*. Their singing was as soft as a baby's lullaby, but had a lot of feeling. The brother prayed over me. Then it happened. I was baptized in the name of Jesus Christ.

My whole body was covered from head to toe. When I came up, it felt like fire was in my bosom. The power of God moved up from my belly and traveled right out of my mouth. I started splashing 'round in the water, and my tongue was out of control—got to saying things I know'd not what. I had my eyes closed tight, but I could hear *hallelujahs* yelled throughout the church.

You see, at Mt. Holly people used to practice how to get in a spirit. I remembered seeing girls in the dressing room raising their skirts just enough to show off the bottom of their fancy, frilly slips, and shuffling their feet. They'd practice and practice, 'til they got the rhythm down pat.

One Sunday, two of them girls got up at the same time and did the exact same shout. When they'd finished, they looked at each other, smiled, and winked—they know'd they'd put on a good show.

Another time, a man and woman fell out in the floor together. The man grabbed a hold of the woman's leg and wouldn't let it go. When his wife tried to pull him off, he held on that much tighter.

Mt. Holly had some of the strangest *spirits* floating 'round there, but what happened to me was *for real*.

On the way home, Buck was awfully quiet.

"Are you all right, honey?" I asked.

"I seen something today I ain't never seen before."

"What's that, Buck?"

"Somebody speaking in tongues coming out of the water," he said. "God must be mighty pleased with you."

"What makes you say that?"

"The way you were carrying on. I ain't seen you that happy in a long time."

"I ain't never felt that way before. You think your folks'll be proud of me?"

"I don't know," he said doubtfully. "Daddy ain't really cared much for Bishop Johnson's doctrine."

My mouth dropped open like I'd been shot. "He don't?"

"No."

"Then why does he listen to him every Sunday?"

"Bishop Johnson offers a large reward to anybody who can condemn his doctrine," Buck began, "and Daddy's been trying to get it. But everything Bishop says is backed up with Bible. That doesn't set well with Daddy, especially seeing how he likes to throw 'round his own opinion."

I know'd right then that I would never please them folks. I girded myself up for whatever I had to face. One thing different though, I had new strength stored up inside.

Chapter 15

Intermission

A couple of my little cousins had fallen asleep, and Aunt Nettie left the room to lie them down. The rest of us refreshed ourselves with bathroom breaks and lemonade.

Aunt Jean initiated the cutting of the pineapple cake and lemon meringue pies. We all followed, without any hesitation.

"Mama, you really *stuck your foot* in this cake," Aunt Jean said, licking her chubby fingers.

Complimenting grunts and moans filled the room, as the rest of us sank our teeth into the scrumptious cake.

"Mama, you only fixed one cake?" Uncle Leroy rebuked. "Now, you know better."

Grandma fanned a modest hand at us, but her smile showed the pleasure that rested in her heart.

Cherie, Pat, and I poured refill after refill of water for the adults, as they raved over each crumb of cake and slice of pie. We fetched napkins for those who chose not to lick their fingers. We wrapped tiny pieces of cake for the little ones who had missed their special treat.

"I think this is one of the best family gatherings we've had," I said.

"I agree," Cherie said, putting away the pie plates.

"It sure is," Pat added. "This one ought to last us a long time."

We finally cleaned the kitchen and dining room, returning them back to the immaculate state Grandma preferred.

The intermission was refreshing, yet it didn't quench the hunger of curiosity that lurked in my mind. I turned off the kitchen light and met the warm glow of the fireplace, as I entered the den. I looked around the room at the contented faces of my loving family before I took my seat.

"Grandma, it took a lot of courage for you to make so many changes," Cherie started, "leaving your family, and then switching religions."

"That's right, baby, and the more I listened to Bishop Johnson, the more changing I had to do. I didn't mind it though. The thing got right sweet to me. But Buck's folks grew harder and harder against me."

Chapter 16

Grandma's Story (No More Tobacco)

One day, I heard Bishop preach something I didn't understand. He talked about how smoking cigars was a lust of the flesh. I never thought about it on that wise, but I know'd there was something to it. I decided I'd ask him more about it after service.

"Bishop, I work in tobacco for my father-in-law, and today I heard you preach against it. What must I do?"

"Daughter, tell him the Lord has saved you now, and the Bible says touch not, taste not, handle not unclean things."

His answer was simple, the hard part was figuring out how to tell Mr. Silas. I couldn't find the right moment to talk to him, so I figured I'd just stop going to the field. I know'd he'd come to me sooner or later, especially after I overheard the late night *Bell* talk.

"Emma, did you stop that gal from going to the fiel'?"

"Naw, I thought that was yo' doing, seeing she's getting farther 'long with child."

"She ain't working hard out there. Just gotta tie the 'bacca together, that's all. Looks like she's making decisions 'round here and I ain't gonna have it," Mr. Silas said. "We'll see who's the boss 'round here come morning."

"And who might that be?" Ms. Emma said.

"Well, um…you know…she's supposed to do what *you* want her to. It's my job to make sure she minds ya."

"You got that right. Now, hush yo' talk."

I prayed for courage to face whatever I had waiting for me the next morning.

****

I whispered the name *Jesus,* as I made my way into the kitchen. I had no idea that Mr. Silas would be in there waiting for me.

"Gal, why won't you in those fiel's yesterday?"

I felt strength rise up from my belly. "Mr. Silas, I can't work in tobacco, no more."

"What you talking 'bout?"

"Bishop Johnson said I can't handle unclean things," I said, trying to look him straight in the face.

"Unclean? As much good tobacco done fo' this fambly? That's foolish."

"I's got to stick to what I believe, sir."

"If you was a wife of mines, I'd tell you which end of the road to take," he said.

"Watch yo'self, Silas!" Ms. Emma screeched from the hall.

The whole time Mr. Silas blasted me, he never looked me directly in the eyes. He acted like he was fussing at the ceiling or the floor. He just stormed out of the house.

I never reported back to them fields, and Mr. Silas never said no more to me about it. Nevertheless, Ms. Emma made up for my field work. She had stopped me from chopping wood, since I was so great with child. Instead, she replaced it with something else—cooking.

Course the first time I had to cook, Ms. Emma made sure Mr. Silas was nowhere in sight. I guess because he didn't want me to touch his food.

She left me home alone and told me to have dinner ready by a certain time. She went to pay one of her old neighbors a visit.

I scrambled 'round there searching through the little seasonings she had. I managed to fix some stew beef and gravy with Irish potatoes and carrots. It felt so good cooking, 'til I even made some sweet potato biscuits.

Ms. Emma came home before Mr. Silas, Bill, and

Buck arrived. She put on her apron and dusted flour on it. Then she sprinkled water on her face to look like she'd been sweating in the kitchen. I stared at her like she was plumb crazy. She gave me an eye—I know'd better than to say one word about her act.

We were fetching the dinner plates when Mr. Silas came in. "Good gracious, Emma, you got it smelling mighty good."

That was the first time I ever heard him say anything good 'bout that kitchen. Ms. Emma didn't comment, and I tried to keep from smiling.

Buck came in shortly after Mr. Silas. "Mama, I can smell the food outside. It's making my stomach growl."

"I'm telling you," Bill agreed, "smells just like a restaurant."

Ms. Emma blew like a mad heifer. I turned my head to keep from laughing.

Mr. Silas, Bill, and Buck sat down at the table, while we fixed their plates. It won't long after they tasted the first mouthful before Mr. Silas cried out: "Lawd Jesus, Emma, you done outdone yo'self today sho 'nough! You got some new recipes from Jessie Mae?"

Ms. Emma just rolled her eyes at Mr. Silas.

"Yeah, Mama, these are the flakiest biscuits," Buck said. "Whatever you did, don't change it."

"Mama, I think this is 'bout the best meal you've ever made," Bill added.

I was so tickled, chil'ren, 'til I almost choked over my food, trying not to laugh.

When I looked at Ms. Emma, she done turned so red with anger, 'til she slammed her fork down and left the room.

"What ails you, Emma?" Mr. Silas yelled. "Here I done give you a compliment 'bout your food and you throwing a fit."

He didn't seem to care too much, 'cause he got up and fixed himself another plateful. Bill and Buck didn't waste no time following him.

I was so pleased to have finally done something to satisfy Mr. Silas, but I know'd better than to let him know it was *my* cooking he enjoyed.

Later that night, I could hardly wait to tell Buck that I was the one who'd cooked the food. He laughed so hard, 'til he cried.

"No wonder Mama was so mad. She ain't never got no real praise from Daddy for her cooking. When he did say something good, we all knew he was just trying to get on her good side," Buck said, chuckling. "Bell, you're a real good cook. I'm right proud of you."

"Thank you, Buck, but I know she's gonna really have it in for me now."

"No doubt about that, but don't worry, Daddy's gonna get more than you."

We giggled ourselves to sleep.

****

Ms. Emma couldn't go on for long trying to fool Mr. Silas, and he couldn't go on for long acting like he enjoyed the food on the days she cooked. I must say, it seemed like he tried real hard to fool her. I guess I done proved myself with cooking 'til he didn't say nothing 'bout me doing it. I just kept up the housework and cooking, 'til time for me to have Willis, Jr.

Me and Buck were right proud of our first son; we took a trip to see my folks. Hattie and Amos went 'long, too. Their son was only a couple months older than ours.

I was still a little scared 'bout seeing Ma and Pa, but glad I didn't have to face 'em alone. When we first got there, Lena met us at the door—tears sprang to her eyes. Ma stood behind her. Her face melted into sweetness when she first glanced at Willis, Jr.

We all hugged for a long time out there on the porch. We finally went inside and sat in the front room. Ma held both babies in each arm, just as proud as a grandma could be. It took awhile for Pa to join us. When he did, the air got stiff—hard to breathe, if I was even breathing. He didn't say much at first. I guess after he'd seen how well me and Hattie looked, and them plump babies sitting on Ma's lap, he soon warmed up a bit, too.

Overall, it was a right nice visit. I could tell they all missed us. Being 'round them, showed me how much I missed them, too.

Felt like my heart would break when we had to leave. I'll never forget that moment. Ma and Lena had great, big smiles on their faces, waving from the porch. Pa stood with his hands resting in his pockets. The corners of his lips bent up slightly into a faint smile—it was a peaceful look—a look that brought tears to my eyes for many nights after.

Buck took me and the baby visiting fambly near 'bout every other weekend. It was on one of them visits that I first met his sister, Phyllis, and brother, Roy. They both lived in Williamston. I looked forward to finally meeting somebody outside of Mr. Silas, Ms Emma, and Bill.

It was a peaceful drive. I didn't know quite what to expect. When we got there, Phyllis gave me the warmest welcome.

"So this is your new bride?" she said, hugging me tight. "I wish you would've brought her to see me before now, but at least I get a chance to see the little one, too."

After she *ooohed* and *aaahed* over the baby, she studied my face for a long time. "My God, Buck, her eyes remind me of—"

"I know, Phyllis, I know," Buck said, giving her a warning look.

She understood and changed the subject. "No need to stand out here, Roy'll be here soon." She nudged me in the back. "Let's go inside so y'all can rest some."

It won't long before Roy walked in, giving us a right cordial greeting, too. We had the most pleasant visit with them—I hated to go home.

The visiting slowed down, and I got back into my old routine. I was hoping we would have our own place after the baby was born, but things moved real slow.

I guess we must have taken too long for Mr. Robert Lee Jones, 'cause he decided to sell the house to somebody else. On top of that, the babies started coming so fast, 'til Buck had to start using the money he had saved for our house. It seemed like I was being buried alive. I spent many days and nights praying for God to deliver me. One day, He answered my prayers.

I was over the washtub, scrubbing and praying, when Buck came home early from the store.

"I got some news for you, baby doll," he said, running over to me.

Course I was surprised to see him that time of the day. I dried my hands on my apron and stood up before he got to me. That man done snatched me up and started spinning me 'round in circles.

"What's done got into you?" I said, giggling like a schoolgirl.

He put me down and got on one knee, like a real gentleman. "I'm gonna finally give you what you deserve. I'm gonna build us a house from ground up."

"What're you talking 'bout, Willis Steele?"

"Daddy's giving us the plot of land across from the tobacco field," he said. "He decided to clear it out, except for the old barn. He's gonna keep that to store small farm equipment and tools."

I could hardly believe my ears. "What made him want to do that?"

"Well, I had asked him 'bout that plot awhile back. I can't prove it, but I think Mama may have had a little to do with it."

"Knowing your mama, she had everything to do with it," I said matter-of-factly.

"No doubt about that, but all I care about is making you happy," Buck said, pulling me close.

I felt like the happiest woman in the world. Prayer was changing things.

Chapter 17

Our History

Grandma rested her head on the back of the rocker and closed her eyes. I figured she was still meditating on those happy moments she shared with Pa-Pa and how she had prayed. Nobody dared to speak. I hated the silence. I didn't know what to do, and I felt awkward sitting there staring at her. It wasn't that I was afraid of religious people; I just didn't want to intrude on their connection with God.

How could everybody sit so calmly? Maybe they were focusing on something to pass the time. I concentrated on my thumbs, spinning them around each other, while I rocked my legs in and out. It was working, until I bumped Pat.

"Quit it," she whispered.

"Sorry, I didn't know—"

"Yeah, chil'ren, prayer surely changes things," Grandma said, reviving from her nostalgia.

I was so glad to hear her voice—my nerves settled down.

"God really blessed me with more than I could even ask or think," Grandma concluded.

"Grandma, I knew how special this house was, but now I can really feel the importance of why Pa-Pa built it," Cherie added.

"Yeah, it's a combination of you and him," Pat started, "your prayers and his love."

"That's right, chil'ren. This house was the start of the Steele's fambly unity. Me and your Pa-Pa meant for it to continue."

That's why I felt so secure at Grandma's. All our history, hopes, laughter, and sorrows were preserved within the walls. I wondered if what was happening between Cherie and Pat was being recorded, waiting to be played back to our children one day.

I scanned the room from the ceiling to the floor, as if I was seeing it for the first time. My mind was twirling with all kinds of thoughts and questions. "How long did it take Pa-Pa to build this house?"

"It took a few years for him to finish. Had to work on it when he could," Grandma said, joining me in glancing around the room.

"I guess knowing you were having this house built, made things a little easier, huh?" Pat asked.

"Not exactly, baby."

Chapter 18

Grandma's Story (Meeting Ruby)

Bill was the carpenter in the fambly. He was happy to hear 'bout us building a house near him. I can't prove it, but it seemed like he decided to settle down with a wife 'round that time, too.

He brought that girl that he told us about by the house one day. We all know'd she was coming, so Ms. Emma made sure I cleaned things up, and that Mr. Silas and Buck were home early. I had cooked a nice meal, so all we had to do was wait.

I was looking out of the kitchen window when Bill drove up. He walked 'round the side of the car and opened the door. Out stepped one of the prettiest girls I'd ever seen. I know'd right away that she'd meet Mr. Silas' approval.

Ms. Emma shooed Buck and Mr. Silas out of the kitchen, I guess so it wouldn't look like we were sitting 'round waiting. She went to the kitchen sink and acted busy. I won't used to putting on no shows, so I just stood there and watched 'em walk right in.

"How're you doing, Bell," Bill said, holding the door open.

"Just fine," I said.

The girl greeted me with a friendly smile, as she walked in so prissy-like. She stepped aside to let Bill in.

"This is Ruby," he said. "Ruby, this is Buck's, wife."

"Pleasure to meet you," she said, extending her dainty hand.

"Likewise," I said, extending mine.

"I'm Bill's mother," Ms. Emma blurted out, barging over to us and nearly knocking me out of the way. "Come into the front room to meet the fambly." She took Ruby by the arm and pulled her along.

We all joined Mr. Silas and Buck in the den. Mr. Silas was holding a newspaper in front of his face, while Buck fumbled with the radio.

"Silas, Buck, this here is Ruby," Ms. Emma announced.

Mr. Silas peeked up, and Buck turned around, both giving a surprised look. It seemed like Mr. Silas' eyes went goo-goo, and I watched Buck's real close to make sure his didn't. They stood up to greet her.

"Mighty nice to meet you, *Miss* Ruby," Mr. Silas said, almost bowing before her. "Why don't you have a seat?"

Ruby and Bill sat on the settee, while Ms. Emma took a seat near Mr. Silas. Buck fetched a chair from the kitchen for me to sit near him. I was glad to know I still had his attention.

"Well, Miss Ruby," Mr. Silas started, "Bill tells me you from Ahoskie. Who's some of yo' people?"

"My Daddy's people are the Jacksons," Ruby started in a soft voice, "but my Mama's people are Lumbee Indians from Robeson County, the Dials."

"Injun, you say?" Mr. Silas asked, with raised eyebrows, scooting to edge of his chair.

Ruby snickered a little, "Yes, sir."

"I believes my wife got a lil Injun in her, too," he said. "Ain't that right, Emma?"

"Naw," Ms. Emma said dryly.

"Anyhow, I guess me and my boy gots the same taste," he said, giving a sly laugh.

"Humph," Ms. Emma said quietly.

Mr. Silas didn't pay her no mind, just kept right on talking.

"Y'all Injuns sho do have a nice grade of hair and some mighty pretty—"

"Will you be having supper with us, Ruby?" Ms.

Emma said, shooting up from her chair. Her foot eased on top of Mr. Silas', and it seemed as though she was pressing that bony foot with all her might. Mr. Silas' grin showed a hint of pain, as Ms. Emma twisted and turned.

"Yes, ma'am, thank you," Ruby said, looking mighty relieved to be free from Mr. Silas' gawking.

"Bell, make sure you set a place at the table for Ruby," Ms. Emma ordered.

"Yes, ma'am," I said, feeling just like a house slave.

Ruby didn't eat much, as I figured, judging by her size. She ate right mannerly. She only used one hand, with the other one resting in her lap. She wiped her mouth after every few bites. I could tell she had a good upbringing.

"So, tell me how you and Bill met," Ms. Emma said.

"Through my cousin, Lawrence, ma'am. He and Bill worked on the same building crew a year ago," Ruby said.

"Lawrence told me about a contracting job in Ahoskie," Bill added. "Being so far away, he invited me to stay over. We had supper at his aunt's house, which happened to be Ruby's mama. We've been keeping company ever since."

Ruby seemed eager to switch the talk away from her and Bill. "So how did you and Buck meet, Bell?"

"Through fambly, too. My sister—"

"So, Miss Ruby, what do yo' daddy do for a living?" Mr. Silas said.

"We're a farming family, sir."

"So is we," Mr. Silas said, sticking out his chest. "We owns quite a bit of prop'ty 'round these parts. My brother, Jack, is a big peanut farmer. I's got a large 'bacca farm 'long with my store business. Been thinking 'bout opening another store soon."

Ms. Emma gave Mr. Silas a dirty look. "You can't even handle the one—"

"You's be well-taken care of if you becomes part of the fambly," he continued.

"Thank you, sir," Ruby said, glancing at Bill.

"Bill can take you to the store and teach you some things," Mr. Silas added. "I'm sure the customers wouldn't mind seeing a fresh, pretty face behind the counter."

"I thank you for the kind offer," Ruby said, blushing, "but I don't know much about business. I wouldn't mind helping out in the field though."

"We's got hired help for the fiel's. Besides, I wouldn't dare think to send such a *nice* daughter-in-law, like yo'self, out there," Mr. Silas said, grinning foolishly.

My head turned real slow in his direction. Buck must have seen the look on my face, 'cause he tapped my leg. I came back to myself.

After dinner, Ruby helped me clear the table. She offered to help with the dishes, but her pretty, little hands were spared by Mr. Silas.

It seemed that Ms. Emma was gonna burst from her sweet-and-quiet wife act. "Bill, I reckon you better take Ruby home. It ain't proper to keep a gal out too late."

No sooner than Bill and Ruby had left, Ms. Emma smacked Mr. Silas across the head. "Put yo' eyes back in yo' head, Silas! You been grinning like a possum all night. Just showed yo'self." She stormed down the hall.

Mr. Silas followed her, rubbing his head. "Sorry, Emma."

****

I thought about Ruby a lot after that—would've been nice having a friendly face around. She seemed to have had a working spirit. I could've really used some grown folks help 'round there. I worked to the point that my own chil'ren took pity on me at times.

When they seen me real tired, they'd tell me to sit down in the old rocking chair on the back porch, while they pumped me some water to drink. Ms. Emma didn't seem to like that one bit.

"It's a shame how you work them chil'ren like lil slaves," she said, as I came in from the porch one day.

"My chil'ren cares 'bout me, Ms. Emma."

"They's making you mo' lazy is all they doing," she said.

I didn't believe in having grown folks talk 'round

chil'ren, so I didn't say nothing more to her—just moved on to another chore.

After that, it seemed like she got real interested in my youngest girl, Paula. She gave her candy from time to time and kept her from doing outside work like the other chil'ren.

Paula usually helped me tend the garden—pulling weeds and picking bugs off the plants. On my gardening days, Ms. Emma said she needed her inside, so I tended my garden alone. I kept myself company by humming and singing. I got so wrapped up in my songs, 'til I didn't hear nobody walk up.

"Bell, Mama said come here."

I recognized the voice, but was shocked to see Paula standing before me. My forehead stung from the frown I made.

"*What* did you call me? And *who* said come here?'

Fear jumped on her face. "G-G-Grandma t-t-told me to call you B-B-Bell and to call her M-M-Mama," she said, gulping and moving from side to side.

Chil'ren, it took all the Holy Ghost I had to stay calm. Ms. Emma was waiting in the kitchen when I opened the door. "Did you send Paula out for me, Ms. Emma?"

"I sure did. I got some mending for you to do, so leave that garden alone," she said.

"Yes, ma'am," I started, "but before I touch one stitch, there's something else I got to mend."

Ms. Emma looked at me like she dared me to say another word. My Ma taught me not to sass grown folks— said something bad would happen to me. I couldn't see nothing worse happening to me than the mess I was already in, so I took my chances. I tried to be as respectful as I could though.

"Ms. Emma, I can put up with a lot of things put on me and a lot of things taken away. But one thing I ain't gonna have is for my chil'ren to call me anything but mama. I birth 'em into this world and I'm the one raising 'em. You're the grandma and that's all you're due."

I didn't give her time to unpart her pinched lips. I turned around and walked out. I guess them evil eyes watched me 'til I got out of sight.

My standing up to Ms. Emma just added fat to the fire. She got that much more evil, if that was possible. The one good thing that happened 'long then was when Bill finally married Ruby.

She was just as sweet as I thought. She often came by during the day, while Bill was working. Her little hands fooled me; they worked right 'long with mine. We started getting close—too close for Ms. Emma.

One day, she offered to take Ruby 'round to see some of her old neighbor friends. I was left at the house, just me and the chil'ren. The phone rang. I never talked on it before—was a little torn 'bout answering it—I figured I'd better.

"Hello," I said in a shaky voice.

"Hey, Bell, you just the one I wanted to talk to. How you doing, girl?" It was Hattie.

A burst of energy ran through me. "Fine, surprised to hear from you. Anything wrong?"

"You ain't never gonna stop being so scary, is you? Ain't nothing wrong. Just called to tell you something."

"What? Are you having another baby?"

"Thank goodness, no," she said. "Will you hush up so I's can talk? I called to tell you 'bout the gas stoves they got out now."

"Gas stoves? I ain't never heard of such."

"Me and Amos went to town last week and I seen 'em. They're mighty nice. Won't have to chop no mo' wood. Folks say they cook just as good or better."

"'Bout how much do they cost?"

"The ones I seen was 'round a hundred and fifty dollars," she said.

My heart sank. "That's too much for me, Hattie. I ain't got that kind of money, and Buck's doing all he can to get us a house."

"I ain't sitting on no gold mine either, but I ain't 'bout to let that stop me. I's gonna find a way to get me one of them gas stoves."

"You've always been strong-headed. Now how are you fixing to do that?"

"I already started saving money. I's been selling my homemade preserves, cakes, and pies. So far, I's got fifteen dollars," she boasted. "It ain't much, but it's a start."

"I ain't got time to even think about selling no pies and things."

"You got a nice garden 'round there. You could sell some of your vegetables," she said.

"You always make things sound so easy," I said. "I guess ain't no harm in trying."

"Just let me know when you want to go to town. We can pick our stoves out together."

The only ones I told were my chil'ren. They started doing little odd jobs for some of the neighbors, to make money. We all kept it our secret.

I sold vegetables from my garden, and the boys shelled peas and sold them in quart jars when we went to town.

Finally, we had enough money for a stove. Me and Hattie went to town and picked out the ones we wanted. They even offered to deliver it. I was so anxious to surprise the fambly.

****

Mr. Silas just happened to be home the day the stove was delivered. I was bubbling inside. He and Ms. Emma were in the back talking, when the delivery truck drove up the path. I opened the door, so they wouldn't have to knock.

As quiet as I tried to be, them deliverymen made a ruckus coming in. Their voices carried all the way to the back and brought Mr. Silas and Ms. Emma right to the kitchen. I thought they would be happy to see something 'round there to make things better. Ms. Emma raised the devil.

"Oh, Silas," she said, grabbing the sides of her head like she was gonna faint. She put on a real show. Scrunching and scooting like the stove was an animal 'bout to bite her. "Bell done got a gas stove. I'm so 'fraid of it…it might blow up. I don't want that thing in here. Make 'em take it 'way, Silas, make 'em take it 'way."

It hardly ever was a time when Ms. Emma let Mr. Silas have any authority, so he walked up to the men with his chest stuck out.

"You hear what my wife said?" he said. "This here is my place of business. The bess thing for you to do is to pack that thing up and take it on 'way from here!"

The deliverymen looked at me. I nodded. I watched them take the stove away, fighting back tears of hurt and anger.

As soon as they left, the show was over. Mr. Silas and Ms. Emma laughed a wicked laugh. I didn't give them the satisfaction of seeing me cry. I swallowed my hurt and spoke softly: "My Ma and Pa always told me to mind how I treat folks, 'cause you never know who's gonna give you your *last drink of water*."

Cold, blank looks crossed their faces and cut their laughter in two.

I left to gather my firewood and I cooked one of the best meals I'd cooked in a long time.

****

I asked Hattie to take me to town the first chance she got. I wanted to see if I could get my money back. She waited outside, while I walked inside the store.

"Here comes the *stove* lady," a man yelled out.

The men standing 'round started laughing with him. I felt my heart beat faster and my face burn, but I didn't drop my head. I walked toward a man in a suit, standing behind the counter.

"I wanted to know if I could get my money back," I said, without cracking a smile.

"Yes, ma'am," he said kindly. "I know them Steeles. What happened didn't surprise me none."

He opened the register and handed me my money. "If you decide to get a stove, just come back to see us," he said, smiling.

I managed to smile, too. "Yes, sir, I will."

I walked out the door with my head high. I was mighty down 'bout not getting my stove, but I wouldn't let

Mr. Silas and Ms. Emma see it. I was glad to find out that Bishop Johnson was coming back through North Carolina. I could hardly wait for Sunday to come, 'cause I know'd he would preach something to give me more strength.

Sure enough, when Sunday came 'round, me and Buck went to see him at the Williamston church. He preached a message that sent a flow of faith right to my heart.

"God sees you. He knows what you're going through. He's watching over you. He won't suffer you to be tempted above that which you're able to bear. It's trying, but you're able. It's testing, but you're able...Somebody went on, you keep going."

I meditated on his message over and over again. I decided to try something different. Whenever things happened that I didn't like, I'd break out into my song: *Victory Shall Be Mine.*

I got to singing that song so much, 'til I could feel it working. One night, as I laid in bed, I heard another *Bell* conversation through the wall.

"Emma, I don't know what to think 'bout that gal. Ever' time I fuss at her, she starts to humming. We better be careful, she might be one of God's least ones."

"If she's anything at all, she would be the least," Ms. Emma said. "You ain't nothing but a weak-knee, jelly-back anyhow. I ain't 'fraid of her."

I didn't bother telling Buck 'bout what I was going through—it was too much anyhow. I just kept praying. Our late night talks were mainly about his progress on the house. I was glad when he told me we'd be moving in a few months.

I wanted to holler with joy, but I held it in reserve. I know'd I would need some of that joy to get me through my *Ms. Emma* days.

Chapter 19

A Solemn Moment

Grandma closed her eyes and hummed, swaying from side to side. The expression on her face looked as if the melody was conceived in the depths of her heart. Each note produced a deeper feeling, until they gracefully emerged from her lips:

"Victory, victory shall be mine.
I know victory, victory shall be mine.
If I hold my peace, let the Lord fight my battle;
Victory, victory shall be mine."

That familiar song, we had heard Grandma sing for years, took on a new meaning. A meaning of strength and courage. It would never be the same again.

Grandma's deep, cotton-field voice pricked my heart—forcing me into spiritual meditation. The entire family swayed in unison to her wavy rhythm. She finished her second round of the song, leaving a surge of power in the room.

I folded my arms tightly across my chest, trying to hold myself together. I felt like I would explode. It seemed that Grandma was taking a puzzle of our family apart: focusing on each piece separately, so we could understand the whole picture.

I always accepted my family at face value, not understanding the labor of love that was behind it. So much taken for granted that could have been so different. Much different and much worse if it wasn't for the integrity Grandma had to hold on through the tough times.

Once the puzzle was fitted together, I knew I would see the picture in a different light. No more dividing seams between each piece. Grandma was placing each part seamlessly with its connecting piece. The final picture wouldn't be the same. It couldn't be. It had to be better.

I could only imagine the hurt she had felt after having her dreams stepped on. My own heart began to ache. I could feel the sorrow grip my chest and creep up toward my throat. I didn't want to cry, not while looking into the face of such a strong, brave woman retelling her sufferings. *But how could I not?* The process had already started. My eyes began to sting.

"Did you ever get a chance to get that gas stove, Grandma?" Cherie whispered, rescuing my emotions.

I was able to blink my eyes dry and swallow the lump that had settled in my throat.

Grandma gave a sweet, victory smile. "I did. A mishap brought that stove back."

Chapter 20

Grandma's Story (The Fall)

I usually did my washing at the creek, which was a good distance from the house. Ms. Emma made a habit of coming down there to stand over me and nag. That made me take a tight hold of them clothes and slam 'em hard against the washboard—satisfying the urge I had of knocking her out. Them clothes always came out nice and clean.

One particular washday, Ms. Emma took a long time to come. Instead, a couple of my chil'ren came running like fire was on their heels.

"Mama, Mama, come quick!" they yelled.

"Grandma was coming out of the house," Willis, Jr. said, catching his breath. "When she started for the steps, she fell. Her leg is all bent up underneath her, and she's hollering something terrible."

"Mama, please hurry, it looks like she's gonna die," Jean added, tugging at my sleeve.

Seemed like my heart jumped into my throat. I ran toward the house. Her screams sent chills down my back. I found her just like they had said. Her face was as red as a strawberry, with agony all over it. I reached out to her; she screamed even louder and waved her hands at me. I sent Willis, Jr. across the tobacco field, to Bill's house. Thank God, he was there. He came right over and gently picked her up. She screamed even more, but he managed to get her in the car and took her to the hospital.

She had broken her hip and had to stay in a

wheelchair. There I was, with all the housework, gardening, and cooking. Not to mention, taking care of her needs, too. I didn't complain—just did the best I could.

Mr. Silas had the cheapest look on his face every time he sat down at the table to eat. Not only were my *black* hands cooking for him, but they were the only ones to serve him, too. He never thanked me, but I figured he was grateful.

One morning, I needed more wood for the stove. I went out back to chop. To my surprise, I found a neat pile stacked on the porch. I couldn't figure out when Buck found the time to do it. After I had thanked him, he told me he hadn't—Mr. Silas had.

He never said nothing to me, but I had to thank him. I saw him walking toward the barn that evening. I ran after him. "Mr. Silas, I want to thank you for chopping that wood for me."

"Uh huh," he said, without turning around to face me.

He kept that up every time I needed wood.

One day, as I was shoving wood into the stove, I heard heavy footsteps come up behind me. It was Mr. Silas. He stood there so quiet, 'til I started feeling a little uneasy.

"D-Do you need me for something, Mr. Silas?"

He seemed to break out of whatever had a hold of him. "B-Bell…my wife said…umm…you can…you can go 'head and get that gas stove if you want to."

He turned to leave, as quickly as he showed up.

"Thank you, Mr. Silas," I yelled after him, "and Ms. Emma, too."

****

Having that stove sure made it a lot easier for me, especially since I had to make sure the house stayed ready for company.

Ms. Emma's accident sure made the fambly come. Reminded me of buzzards 'round a kill—get their fill and move on. Everybody had a good appetite. It was during that time that I found out that lil Ruby was a good hand in the kitchen.

She was right faithful coming over early in the morning with big pots of food. She did all she could to help me. I was grateful.

On one of the fambly visits, I got the chance to meet Buck's sister, Martha. They called her Sissy. To my surprise, she didn't live too far from us. I'd never seen her before then though.

Sissy looked and acted a lot like Ms. Emma. She was just a tad bit nicer. She came 'round once a week to see 'bout her mama. She didn't seem to want to do much work. Just talked and ate more than anything.

Phyllis and Roy came by 'bout every two weeks. They really made themselves useful. She helped me 'round the house, while Roy played with the chil'ren. It seemed like she always had something she wanted to say, but never did.

"Bell, it feels like you're my blood sister at times," she said. "I wish y'all lived closer to us."

"Maybe after Buck gets the house finished, y'all can come stay with us sometime."

"I'd like that a whole lot," she replied, smiling.

Although most of the fambly favored Ruby, Phyllis and Roy seemed right attached to me.

The visiting went on for a while, and then slowly stopped. Even Ruby stayed away. I guess she needed time to rest—never thought her first few months of married life would start like mine: with hardships.

It didn't take Ms. Emma long to get used to being in her wheelchair. She went right back to her nagging ways.

"Bell, did you dust this furniture 'round here," she said, running her hand across one of the tables in the front room.

"Yes, ma'am, I sure did."

"It's 'bout time for this floor to be wiped down."

"I did it this morning."

"When was the last time you washed these curtains in here?"

"Yesterday, ma'am."

"They needs to be ironed."

"I did it before I hung 'em."

"These windows could stand a cleaning," she said, smearing her fingerprints across the bottom of the glass.

"I did them, but I'll clean where you just touched if you like," I said, hoping she would leave me alone.

"This house would stay clean if I won't in this wheelchair," she said, wheeling herself down the hall.

I know'd she won't never one to do much 'round the house. It seemed like being in that wheelchair brought out more fault finding. I managed the best I could to stay on top of things. It didn't help none, 'cause what she couldn't find, she'd make up something to fuss about.

One day, a close friend of hers came by. Her name was Miss Eva Perkins. She was a pleasant lady. She complimented me on my work around the house.

"Emma Faye, it looks like you's being taken care of right well. Yo' skin looks so fresh. Sure is a blessing to have such a nice daughter-in-law to take such good care of things."

"I's coming 'long all right, considering," Ms. Emma said, whining. "Still not the same as doing things for yo'self."

"I can imagine," Ms. Eva agreed, "but Bell's doing a mighty fine job. Everything looks and smells so clean and fresh."

Though it didn't come too often, a little praise sure lifted my spirits—Ms. Emma know'd just how to kill 'em.

After that visit from Miss Eva, Ms. Emma would send back half-eaten plates of food. I couldn't prove it, but it seemed like she wanted to lose weight, so she wouldn't look so well-cared for.

I thought that was bad enough, but bless my God, something worse happened not long after.

I was walking down the hall, and a foul odor hit me when I passed her door. At first I thought the chil'ren forgot to empty the pots that morning. I checked each room, and all of 'em had been emptied. I knocked on Ms. Emma's door.

"Who's there?" she hollered.

"It's Bell, may I come in?"

"Fo' what?"

"I need to check something," I said, pushing the door open.

The smell hit me like somebody knocking the breath out of me. When I checked her pot, it was empty. The smell was strong in the room. I followed it to her bed. I found it, too—right on her. The woman had started wetting and messing on herself. She found a way to kill all my fresh, clean smells.

It was mighty strange how she became so helpless all of a sudden. I had another task on my hands.

I mentioned to Buck about how his mama was half eating, and how she had started soiling things.

One evening, I was walking down the hall to her room with some warm water, to give her a bath. I saw her door closed and heard talking inside. Buck and Mr. Silas were in the room talking to her 'bout not eating and all. What that woman done told them, could've made a rattlesnake's blood boil.

"Buck, Silas…I didn't want to say nothing…but seeing how y'all come to question me, I feel like I's got to tell the truth," Ms. Emma said, sounding so pitiful. She could've made a heart of stone crumble. "I's been so hungry 'round here, I don't know what to do. That gal don't half feed me…just going 'round like she's the woman of this house and leaves me back here all alone."

I was so shocked and mad, 'til I almost dropped the basin of water.

"I reckon she wants me to go 'head and die," she said. "I tries not to bother her, but I's so weak…I soil my things."

She had the nerve to burst into a crying fit, like somebody at a funeral.

My temples pounded. I turned around and went outside on the porch. It felt like hot pins were sticking in my head. I stood on the porch awhile, to cool myself down.

It won't long before Mr. Silas came raging. "Gal, I come to tell you a thing or two—"

"Daddy, that's *my* wife," Buck said, rushing behind him and grabbing his arm. "I'll talk to her 'bout Mama."

Mr. Silas hesitated a bit, turned to leave, and then changed his mind. "As much as my wife done for you," he said, pushing Buck out of the way. "Taking you in like one of her own daughters. You ain't got enough respect for her to even feed her and keep her clean? I know'd you won't good for nothing!"

"Please, Daddy, I'll talk to her," Buck said, stepping between us.

Mr. Silas finally left. I never looked up at him or Buck—just stood there, while my insides felt like they were gonna burst wide open.

"Be strong, Bell," Buck said, gently pulling my chin up. My eyes met his. He stared at me a long time, like he saw something deeper than just my eyes.

He cupped my cheeks in his rough hands—they gave me comfort. "I know they're hurting you," he started, "but for my sake, be strong…please…be strong." His voice shook, then broke—he hugged me real tight. I felt warm tears slip down my neck. I held him tight, too. That night, we shared the same pain.

Chapter 21

Reliving the Pain

Grandma's pain was so fresh. So real. So alive. I felt another lump rise up in my throat, making it hard to swallow. I did a short series of blinks to fight back the tears. Judging from the expressions on their faces, Cherie and Pat seemed to have had the same battle I did—resisting the cry. The rest of the family sat solemnly, with cast-down eyes.

Grandma's strength amazed me. "How'd you do it, Grandma," I whispered.

Grandma took a cleansing breath. "By the grace of God, child."

"It must have been hard for you to take care of her after lying on you," I said.

"By that time, baby, I had already learned to take it as it comes."

"How could she look at you? Didn't she at least feel guilty?" Pat asked, using her hands to express herself.

"Guilt seemed to have been the farthest thing from her mind…at least at that time," Grandma said, sighing.

"How did you feel the next time you had to face her?" Cherie asked.

"I had to tell myself that they lied on Jesus. Who am I to be lied on? When I thought on that, I started feeling better."

"Grandma, you're a real saint," I added.

"Well, baby, there's always gonna be something to test you. If you can stand the test, that'll prove if you're a real woman."

I nodded, trying to comprehend the meaning behind what she said. *Were the issues between Cherie and Pat a test? Making real women out of all of us? Who decides these tests? Or do they just happen?*

"Now, that don't mean that it'll be easy. One thing's for sure, they're bound to come, whether you want 'em to or not," she continued.

Grandma always knew what to say and when to say it. I always thought her wisdom was just a part of being old. I never knew wisdom came with such a bitter price—the hardships of life.

I wasn't sure if I was ready for the tests that were coming to prove my womanhood. If turning out like Grandma would be the end result, I guess it would be worth it.

Was there a way to prepare for tests? Do you have to study for them like the ones in school?

"Prayer was the only thing I had to help me face each day," Grandma whispered.

"What happened after that?" I asked.

"Something kind of strange," Grandma said, chuckling. "Little gloves started popping up 'round the house."

Uncle Leroy startled us with a deep laughter. "Oh, Mama, you ain't never gonna let me forget that, huh?"

"How can I?" she replied. "That's what added fuel to my fire. How 'bout you tell that part?"

"You know I ain't good at talking like you are," Uncle Leroy said, shaking his head disapprovingly.

"Son, it won't have the same feeling if I told it. It gots to come from the horse's mouth, no matter how good or bad it is."

"Well, if you insist," Uncle Leroy said, before clearing his throat several times.

Chapter 22

Uncle Leroy's Story
(The Gloves)

Mama's gas stove started it all. I'd seen all the different ways we had made money—that gave me an idea.

"Mama, do you mind if I sell some butter beans, so I can get a shotgun?" I asked.

"What's wrong with the one your daddy gave you?"

"It's sometimey. Sometimes it work and sometimes it don't. It got jammed up on me the last couple of times I took it out—made me miss two rabbits."

"Well, y'all helped me get something to help the fambly. I reckon your hunting'll help, too," she said.

"Thank you, Mama."

I had started selling butter beans and doing little odd jobs for folks. I wasn't making much, but I was encouraged.

After Grandma broke her hip, Mama needed me at home. I was always a little afraid of Grandma because she became meaner and meaner after her fall. I was glad Willis, Jr. was the one who had to wheel her around the yard, instead of me. I was satisfied with taking and fetching her plates of food.

I'd seen all the trouble Mama went through trying to get her to eat. I remember sitting outside Grandma's door, waiting for Mama to come out.

"Can I eat Grandma's food if she doesn't want it?"

"You already ate, boy. It's a sin to be greedy," Mama said, frowning.

"I just don't want it to go to waste," I said, trying to

justify myself.

"It won't. Maybe she'll eat it later."

"If she doesn't want it later, can I have it then?"

"Leroy, this here is your grandma's food. I've got to make sure she eats it, or it'll be more trouble for me. Do you understand?" she said, looking like she was about to cry. "I don't need no trouble from you. Just do like I say, boy."

After that tongue-lashing, I tried to do whatever I could to help Mama more with taking care of Grandma— until the first time she soiled herself.

Mama called Willis, Jr., Jean, Margaret, and me into the room. She wanted Willis, Jr. and me to take all the soiled things out to the washtub by the creek, while Jean and Margaret helped her clean Grandma up.

As soon as I entered the room, it felt like my insides started creeping up my throat. I tasted a bitter acid in my mouth. I tried to keep swallowing to push everything back down. Before I knew anything, I had to be cleaned up, too. I never knew my stomach was so weak, until then.

Vomit gushed down the front of my shirt, leaving a puddle at my feet. The sight of it, called for more. My stomach pumped out of control—it was like it had a heartbeat of its own. With each tug, more and more splashed on my pants, shoes, and anything in its path. I got to the point where my stomach kept tugging, but nothing came out.

Mama stayed calm through it all. She had Willis, Jr. take me out of the room. Poor Jean and Margaret had to stay and help. I was the youngest boy, and I wanted to prove myself. I was so embarrassed when Mason had to take my place. It was hard to keep my mouth from watering every time I thought about how Grandma's room smelled.

Henry stayed with me. He helped me change my clothes. Willis, Jr. and Mason got all the soiled things, including my stuff. Mason used his top lip to plug his nose. He reminded me of some of the fish I'd caught. It was a funny sight, but as soon as he got near me, I got a whiff of the things he was carrying. My stomach started jerking, and I started gagging.

Willis, Jr. offered me a little advice: "Leroy, maybe you need to come outside with us. The fresh air might help."

It did help. I was able to start the fire for Mama's boiling pot—those things needed a real scalding.

Mama had expected Grandma's soiling to be an on-going thing, so she prepared herself. I, on the other hand, had some decisions to make. I didn't have enough money for the shotgun, but it didn't matter too much because something else became more important.

I hated to see Mama suffering with Grandma the way she was. Even though she used a lot of pine cleaners, the odor was like a bad aftertaste: just lingered for a while.

I had started losing weight. Mama questioned me about it. I was afraid to tell her the truth. I figured I'd give her little hints.

"Does anybody know where these here gloves came from?" she asked, fanning rubber gloves over the dinner table. "Seems like everywhere I go, I find 'em. I've got enough to do without having to pick up behind y'all, too."

Nobody said a word.

"Don't y'all hear me talking to you? Where did they come from?"

Still, nobody said a thing. Guilt took a hold of me. Mama always had a way of knowing things anyway...it was no need to lie to her.

"I-I'm the one, Mama," I started, "but I didn't mean for you to pick up behind me. I meant for you to have 'em."

If looks could kill, Mama's eyes would've knocked me out. "What in the world do I need gloves for, boy? Have you ever seen me working in gloves?"

"No ma'am," I whispered, "but you ain't never had to do the kind of work you're doing now, either."

"Leroy, I ain't got time to play foolish games with you. Tell me what these here gloves are for."

I swallowed real hard. "E-Ever since you started cleaning up Grandma...I've been having a hard time...um...eating your biscuits. It's been kind of hard for me to eat period."

Dead silence filled the air—it seemed like

everybody was scared to move. We waited for Mama to blast.

Mama gave me a blank look. Her lips started quivering. Then her body started shaking. She burst out laughing and couldn't stop. Tears rolled down her face. The gloves fell from her hand. She laughed until she bent over the table. Whenever she glanced at the gloves, she laughed harder and harder.

We all just looked at her, wide-eyed. Margaret started giggling. Then all of us started laughing until we bounced up and down in our chairs.

Mama slowly raised herself up. "I know how you feel, baby," she said in between gasps of breath. "It's been hard for me to eat my own food."

We laughed so loud; it reminded me of a bomb going off. Paula fell clean out of her seat.

Willis, Jr., Henry, and Mason all gave me a pat on the back that night. I proved myself after all. Mama had seen how faithful I was, too. I kept her supplied with all the gloves she needed.

Chapter 23

Grandma's Story
(Ms. Emma Goes Away)

Using them gloves made Ms. Emma become right offended with me. Her voice was low and hateful the first time she'd seen 'em.

"You got some nerve actin' scornful of me. I ain't some ole filthy animal!"

She got to the place she didn't want me 'round her—even touching her things. When I tried to give her a bath, she screamed and hollered like I was killing her.

It got so bad, 'til Mr. Silas asked Bill if Ruby could come over to care for Ms. Emma. She did her best, but Ms. Emma was too much for her.

Ruby came into the kitchen one day. Her face was red and full of hurt. I could tell she was 'bout ready to cry.

"Bell, how do you do it?" she asked.

"Do what?"

"Handle her," she said, pointing down the hall.

"I guess I'm 'bout used to it. It's been this way ever since I came into this fambly."

"You're a good one to stay," she whispered.

She sat down at the kitchen table. Tears ran down her face. She didn't make one sound. I took her in my arms like one of my own chil'ren. She buried her face in my chest and cried 'til her eyes ran dry. I felt so sorry for that poor child—she'd been fooled, too.

After that, Ruby didn't come over much at all. It won't long before she and Bill moved away—said work was better 'round the Raleigh area.

When they left, it felt like part of me went with them: some of my hopes.

Ms. Emma didn't get no easier to care for. Still carried on like somebody who had done lost their mind. Mr. Silas hired Miss Eva to come and sit with Ms. Emma from morning to noon, making sure she ate her breakfast and lunch. He was home in the evening for her dinner.

Miss Eva's first visit surely taught Ms. Emma a good lesson. I carried Ms. Emma's breakfast down the hall for Miss Eva—I figured her hands needed to be free, just in case she fell out. Course Ms. Emma won't expecting company, so she hollered at me when I knocked. When I opened the door, it was like walking right into an outhouse.

"Ms. Emma, Miss Eva's here to make sure you eat your breakfast," I said, putting the plate on the nightstand.

Ms. Emma's eyes looked 'bout the size of quarters. "E-E-Eva? I-I didn't know you was comin'. So sorry 'bout all this," she said, sitting up in the bed and brushing the covers.

"This gal don't half care for me and I's so weak...can't do for myself...I-I's so sorry you have to see me like this."

Miss Eva just nodded. I reckoned she was still holding her breath.

Ms. Emma turned a new shade of red: a mixture of shame and hate. "Eva, why don't you wait in the kitchen? Bell's got to get me cleaned up a bit."

She didn't have to say it twice. Miss Eva tore out of the room, gagging all the way up the hall.

I didn't have no more trouble with Ms Emma's morning baths from then on.

One morning, I was gathering clothes for the wash when Ms. Emma stopped me from putting her things in the basket. "Bell, take my clothes to Sissy's house. She'll wash 'em for me."

"Yes, ma'am," I said.

"I's got chil'ren who can look out for my things, since you got a *glove* problem."

"Yes, ma'am," I said, biting my lip to keep from saying more.

The next day, after Miss Eva arrived, I left to take Ms. Emma's clothes to Sissy's house. When I first got there, she greeted me with a nice *hello*. I told her my purpose for coming and after that, I never made it inside.

"I'm not able to do it. You'd just have to take them clothes back," she said, stiff-faced.

She didn't bat an eye. I know'd that was the end of our talk. I made my way back home. I could hardly wait to tell Ms. Emma what Sissy had said, especially in front of Miss Eva.

I placed the basket of clothes on the porch. I was surprised to see Ms. Emma at the kitchen table eating and laughing with Miss Eva.

I guess she won't expecting to see me. Her laughter was cut short. "What you doing back so soon?"

"I brought your clothes back, ma'am."

"Sissy's done with 'em already?"

"No, ma'am. She said she won't able to wash 'em. She told me to bring 'em back."

Ms. Emma's mouth dropped. "Sissy won't wash my clothes?"

"No, ma'am," I replied.

Ms. Emma sat there and cried like a baby. This time it won't no show.

I turned to walk away. Miss Eva stopped me. "Bell, what are you gonna do?"

"I'm gonna wash 'em."

"You're one in a thousand," she praised.

****

Ms. Emma kept going downhill. She still seemed to hold hatred in her heart for me. No matter how hard she tried to avoid me, she couldn't get 'round my help.

She complained to Mr. Silas more and more 'bout me, 'til he finally called one of his daughters in Virginia. I overheard him on the phone one day.

"Annie, your mama's real sick, and Buck's wife don't treat her right 'round here. Figured it'll be better for her to stay with you awhile. Buck'll be bringing her up."

I don't know what Buck's sister said to Mr. Silas, but I remember the end of his conversation with her. "What's all the talk, gal? That's yo' mama. You ought to want to help her...don't tell me 'bout Lonnie, he's the one who took you so far 'way from home. He should've thought about that before he married you."

By the weekend, Mr. Silas had gathered up Ms. Emma's things and drafted my oldest girl, Jean, to go 'long to help Annie out.

Buck hated to leave because he was putting the finishing touches on our new house. We were planning to move in another week or so. I'd already started packing our things. That setback didn't surprise me none, 'cause that was just Ms. Emma's way: rule or ruin.

When Ms. Emma was away, it won't much I had to do 'round the house. Me and the chil'ren spent a lot of time visiting the new house and tidying up. We enjoyed imagining how things were gonna be. Buck had even put in indoor plumbing, so we didn't have to worry with pumping water. He really tried to give me all that he had promised, I could tell.

****

The time came for us to move. I started unpacking some of the boxes; I ran across a picture of Buck when he was a lot younger. He and a girl were sitting with their arms wrapped around each other. I took a closer look. Buck had the biggest smile. I figured he must have really liked that girl, and I could see why. She had the prettiest, long hair braided just like an Indian's. She could've passed for one, too, if it won't for her color. She was 'bout dark as me. The strangest thing 'bout that picture was that she won't smiling at all. In fact, she looked rather sad. I put the picture back into the box. I'd ask Buck about her, when I felt the time was right.

Things felt mighty homey. A big burden had rolled off me: Ms. Emma was away, Mr. Silas was across the field, and I had my fambly together in *my own* house.

I took it upon myself to cook meals and clean for

Mr. Silas. Whether he appreciated it or not, I didn't know 'cause he never said *thank you* for nothing I done.

'Bout the first few days we were at the new house, I went through some of Buck's things and ran across that picture again.

After dinner, I got enough nerve to ask him about it. "When I was unpacking boxes, I found a picture of you and a young girl sitting together. Do you mind telling me who she is?"

Buck didn't say nothing for a long time. He didn't look mad, so I just sat there and waited 'til he was ready to talk.

"What picture, Bell?"

"I'll go get it if you want."

He was quiet, but he didn't stop me. I left to get the picture. "Here it is," I said, handing it to him.

He slowly took it out of my hand. It seemed like a million things were running through his mind, but he didn't breathe not one.

"That's Ethel," he whispered.

"It looks like you were mighty fond of her," I said.

"I was."

His answer took me by surprise. "Well, who is Ethel?" I said, trying not to sound jealous. "And where is she now?"

Buck took a deep breath and placed the picture on the table. "She passed away not long after this picture was taken."

"Oh," I whispered, in shock.

Buck shifted uncomfortably in his chair. "That's enough questions for now, all right?"

I nodded. I could tell he was real bothered. I let him have his time. Even though I still wanted to know who she was and how she died, I know'd better than to ask.

'Bout a week after we moved in, Hattie and Amos came by to see the new house. They raved about how nice it was. Course Amos got put on the hot seat, being that they had outgrown the little house he'd bought for them.

"This is mighty fine, Bell. Must be nice having all this space," Hattie said, eyeing Amos.

"Yeah, Buck, I didn't know you had building skills in you. You've got to show me a few things, so I can add more rooms to our house," Amos said, responding to Hattie's eyes.

"I'd be glad to," Buck said.

Hattie looked more hopeful. We finished our tour of the place.

That evening, Buck and Amos sat 'round the table laughing and talking after we'd finished the nice dinner me and Hattie had prepared. The chil'ren played in the yard 'til it got dark. Hattie and Amos ended up spending the night. The chil'ren piled up in their rooms, playing 'til they fell asleep. We sat up talking 'bout old times. That was the first fambly gathering in this house.

A few days later, we were at Mr. Silas' house listening to Bishop Johnson on the radio, when the phone rang.

Buck answered it, and I heard disappointment in his voice. "Oh, that's a shame. That's all right, it ain't your fault, that's just Mama. Well, I'll see what I can do…yeah, all right, bye."

Come to find out, Annie couldn't handle Ms. Emma—her own Mama. Ms. Emma was coming back.

Jean had an earful to tell when she finally came home.

Chapter 24

Aunt Jean's Story
(The Crazy House)

I'm not much at telling stories like Mama, but I was the one who had seen it all firsthand. I guess I'm the best one to tell it.

I was around twelve or so when I had to leave. When Mama first told me I had to go to Aunt Annie's house to help with Grandma, I cried and cried. I had never been that far away from home, and I didn't know how long I had to stay. On top of all that, I was almost deathly afraid of Grandma. I felt more protected around Mama.

Once I got to Virginia, I was glad to see that Aunt Annie had a couple of daughters a little older than me. I couldn't understand what they needed me for, but it didn't take long to find out.

Those girls couldn't do a lot of the things Mama had taught me to do. They were on the lazy side, and so was Aunt Annie. After she found out how much I could do, she didn't waste any time handing over chores.

The first week crept by. I was mighty homesick, and I missed Mama's cooking. Aunt Annie had a time taking care of Grandma. They fussed from morning until night.

I thought it was strange for Grandma to treat her own daughter like she treated Mama, but I figured she was set in her contrary way and wasn't changing.

I stayed there for a month. It seemed like a year. The Saturday before I came back home, Aunt Annie went in Grandma's room that morning. Just as fast as she went in, she burst back out and was hollering for me to come quick.

The closer I got to the door, I recognized the smell. I knew what Aunt Annie wanted with me. Grandma had another one of her *accidents*.

I had gotten used to helping Mama clean up Grandma, but that was something totally new for Aunt Annie. She stood over Grandma, fanning her face. Her head started shaking in rhythm with her hands, like she was having some kind of seizure.

"Mama, instead of you making us go through all of this, you can just use a bedpan!" she said.

As swift as a hawk can snatch up a rabbit, Grandma grabbed Aunt Annie around her neck and started choking her. I was so shocked. I felt cold jolts shoot up and down my body, leaving my toes tingling.

Aunt Annie started gagging and turning red. Somehow, I managed to find my voice. "Uncle Lonnie, Uncle Lonnie, come quick. Grandma's killing Aunt Annie!"

Uncle Lonnie bolted in the room and grabbed Grandma's wrists. It looked like he was pressing them with all his might.

Finally, Grandma hollered out and fell backwards on the bed. Aunt Annie held her throat and ran out of the room crying and gasping for air. I had never seen that kind of carrying on in my whole life.

No one dared to enter that room, until it was time to feed her. Of course, they chose *yours truly* to do it. I knew everybody was just as scared as I was. I couldn't understand why they would choose the youngest thing in the house to throw to the lion. I felt like a real sacrifice. I tried to remember the story Mama had told me about Daniel when he was in the lion's den. It helped some.

I must say, Mama didn't raise a dummy. When I went to Grandma's room with her tray of food, I didn't bother knocking. I figured she was asleep, and Lord knows I didn't want to wake her. I put the tray on the floor and slowly opened the door, to keep it from squeaking. When I peeked in, sure enough, she was asleep.

I picked up the tray and tiptoed into the room. I walked around the foot of the bed to the opposite side of where she was lying. I figured if she woke up, she couldn't reach over and grab me. I quietly slid the tray next to her.

I tiptoed to the door. "Grandma, Grandma." She finally woke up and looked at me. "I put your food beside you," I said, closing the door as quickly as I could.

Nothing made me any happier than when Aunt Annie told me I was going back home. I was glad to get out of that crazy house.

Chapter 25

Understanding Great-Grandma Steele

We all looked at Aunt Jean in disbelief. Cherie broke the silence, "It's hard to imagine someone being so evil. What made her that way?"

Grandma directed our attention to her, as she interjected with a subtle, "Well." Only her ingenious mind could answer that question.

"You see, the Bible speaks of the love of money being the root of all evil. Mr. Silas spoiled Ms. Emma to the point of pure selfishness," Grandma said. "She won't interested in him, but she loved money. He fooled her into thinking he had lots of it—the old corncob trick. The last dollar came off after she married him."

"So what happened after that?" Cherie asked.

"Mr. Silas had a good business mind. He made enough money to keep her spoiled," Grandma said.

"That's crazy," Pat said, sucking her teeth. "Marrying for money."

"You're right," Grandma started, "but she looked just the way he wanted: light skin, silky hair and pretty. So he didn't care what her reason was for marrying him. She had to be the center of attention, so as long as she got that, she was happy."

"It seems like they both made a big mistake," I added.

"Yeah, baby, that's right. They both chose selfish things over love. Where there's love, there's understanding. But trouble and peace can't rest in the same place—makes for a miserable life."

The family all nodded, making whispered comments. Love was all our family had ever known. Because of that, we held a bond that remained unbroken.

"Jean, you told that story just like you did all them years ago," Grandma said. "It won't easy for me to hold my joy, knowing Ms. Emma was coming back. Little did I know other trouble was coming, too."

Chapter 26

Grandma's Story (Snakebite)

I didn't know how I was gonna handle two houses. It didn't seem like Mr. Silas could hire nobody to help with Ms. Emma. I reckoned 'bout everybody know'd the trouble that came with her. So I started staying with her during the day, 'til Mr. Silas got home.

I'd have Jean run things at home while I was away. I'd come home 'round noon to get my dinner started, while Ms. Emma was napping. Margaret would sit with her just in case she'd wake up needing something. We did that awhile, but things didn't get no better.

"Bell, I really want to thank you for how faithful you've been by my Mama and Daddy," Buck said. "I was hoping once we moved into our own house, things would be a lot better for us. I didn't know Mama would take a turn for the worse. I know it's putting more of a strain on you though."

"We've got to take the good with the bad," I said, with cast-down eyes. "At least I have a nice home to come back to in the evenings."

Buck know'd me too well. I was just as disappointed with the way things were going as he was.

"I know you were looking forward to us having our own life with our own family," he said, lifting my chin to make my eyes meet his. "And that's all I want, too. I just don't know what to do."

The weight of his burden made his shoulders sag. He sat down in his favorite chair, resting his elbows on his knees. I figured only I could make his burden lighter. Only I could give him hope, even though it meant more suffering for me. I had to do it. For him, for me, for our fambly.

I got on my knees in front of him. "Buck, your daddy gave us this plot of land, which was a mighty nice gesture. I believe your mama had something to do with it, too. If it won't for them, you wouldn't have been able to build this fine house. It's no more than right for them to come live with us."

Chil'ren, Buck's face shone like new money. He hugged me so tight, I could hardly breathe. He looked at me with the most genuine look of love I'd ever seen. "I'm mighty blessed to have you for my wife."

Buck had a long talk with Mr. Silas and Ms. Emma about moving in with us. It was early fall and with winter coming, we had indoor plumbing and better heating. To my surprise, neither one of them objected. I guess they started learning how to swallow some of their pride.

I didn't know what to expect when they finally settled in. But something was different 'bout Ms. Emma. She still kept a sour look on her face, but she didn't have much to say to me. She didn't put up a fight when I tried to feed her. The chil'ren were afraid of her being in our house, especially after Jean came back with her story. But Ms. Emma didn't bother nobody...just had a look 'bout her that made me wonder if she was being tortured in her own mind.

Bill and Ruby had started visiting more and more to check on Ms. Emma. Sometimes Bill would come alone and stay with us for a few days. Buck stayed so busy running the store and trying to do carpentry work on the side, 'til I was right grateful whenever Bill came 'round to give us a hand with things.

On one of Bill's visits, I had the chil'ren raking leaves in the backyard. I needed another rake, so I went 'round to the front of the house. That's when I overheard Mr. Silas and Bill talking.

"It's 'bout time to give that old barn a good cleanin'," Mr. Silas said. "I'm gonna get Buck's boys to go in there and start bringing out the small stuff."

"Daddy, it's been awhile since anybody's been in there. It'll be better for us to do it."

Mr. Silas didn't pay Bill no mind. He started heading 'round back where the chil'ren were. It seemed like a courage came over me like David going against Goliath.

"Mr. Silas," I yelled after him, "I don't want my boys going in that barn."

He straightened his back and never turned 'round to me, just kept walking toward the chil'ren. I took off running, with the rake in my hand. I don't know if Bill thought I was gonna beat his daddy down or what. All I know is that he came running after me.

By the time I reached Mr. Silas, he had Willis, Jr. clutched in one hand and Henry in the other. He was dragging 'em toward the barn. I stood right in front of him and looked him dead in the eyes.

"I don't want my boys going in that barn."

He turned his face from me and looked at the boys. "These boys gonna do what I say do."

"Ain't no telling what's in there," I started, "and they ain't going in."

Bill was there witnessing the whole conversation. He'd seen that both of us were just as stubborn as the other. He stepped between us.

"Daddy, Bell's right. It's not safe to send those children in there without us checking the barn out first."

Mr. Silas shot a threatening look at Bill. "I didn't ask fo' yo' two cents. You rather go against what I say, for this black—"

"Daddy, ain't no need for all that."

"I ain't got time fo' fools," Mr. Silas said, storming away.

I didn't have enough heart to tell Buck how I had sassed his daddy, and I was glad Mr. Silas didn't show up for dinner that evening.

I couldn't sleep well that night. It was a bit warm and things just didn't seem right. I didn't know if it was the heat or my nerves working on me. I tossed and turned. My mind kept rambling. On top of it, I had this eerie feeling. I figured it was 'cause of me standing up to Mr. Silas. I didn't trust him, so I got in prayer...to protect me and the chil'ren. I stayed on my knees 'til I fell asleep.

In the wee hours of the morning, I was jolted from my sleep.

BANG, BANG, BANG. "Buck, Buck, I need you," Mr. Silas yelled through the door.

Buck sprang to his feet. "What is it, Daddy? What's the problem?"

"I need you," Mr. Silas said, sounding more nervous than before. "P-P-Please help me...been bit by a copperhead!"

"Lawd have mercy! I'm coming Daddy...I'm coming. Bell, where are my pants?"

Buck looked like a wild man: spinning 'round in circles, not knowing where to take his first step.

I spotted his breeches on the chair near the door. "Over there," I said, pointing.

His eyes followed my finger. He grabbed his breeches, hopped on one foot 'til he finally forced one leg through. Before he could get the other leg in, Mr. Silas' voice came thundering through the door again.

"Hurry, Buck, f-f-feeling weak...and the pain...the pain hurts something terrible."

"Coming, Daddy, coming."

Buck finally got hisself together and disappeared behind the door. I stayed on the floor, trembling and shaking all over. All the sleep had left me. I got dressed and started my day, not knowing how it was gonna end.

I went to check on Ms. Emma, 'cause with all that commotion, I didn't know what it might have done to her. I opened her door. She was sitting straight up in the bed.

"Ms. Emma, are you all right?"

She didn't say a thing. Just sat there. She didn't blink or nothing. I quietly shut the door. I figured I'd deal with her later. I checked on the chil'ren. Thank God, they were all sound asleep. I was grateful to have time to get my nerves together.

****

Buck, Bill, and Mr. Silas came home hours later. Mr. Silas had his right arm bandaged up. He didn't say a word to me, just walked down the hall to his room.

Buck and Bill took a seat at the kitchen table.

"Daddy came to my room early this morning," Bill started, "wanting to go into the barn. He reached down to move a stack of feed buckets, when he hollered out. A copperhead was curled up behind the buckets and struck him. He stumbled into me, grasping his arm. Then he started squeezing and pumping it, trying to get the bad blood out."

Fear jumped into my heart. All I could think about was how he had wanted to send my boys into that same barn.

"It's a good thing I had an old rag in my back pocket, 'cause that's all we had to wrap his arm with," Bill continued. "I made a tight knot behind the two tiny fang marks where the snake had bitten him. I sent him to the house to get Buck, while I found a hoe. The snake was in the same spot. I was able to kill it and put it in a bucket. We took it to the hospital with us."

It seemed like Bill talked without taking a breath, and I held mine 'til he stopped. I was speechless; all I could do was shake my head in disbelief.

"Good thing you didn't let them boys in there, Bell," Bill said. "A mighty good thing."

Buck gave me a confused look. I didn't feel ashamed. I felt grateful—I had done right.

Chapter 27

Grandma's Story (Final Thanks)

It was a pitiful time going on 'round that house. Ms. Emma was getting worse every day, and after the snakebite, Mr. Silas' arm never did go back to its right size: stayed swollen.

All their chil'ren started coming 'round more—still I was the one who had the burden of taking care of 'em.

Winter was slowly passing by, but it was mighty trying on us. Ms. Emma was eating less and less, and had gotten a nasty cough. She kept that cough 'til March of the following year.

Buck and Mr. Silas were getting more and more worried 'bout her, but I was the one who witnessed it all.

I went into her room one morning, and she called for me in a weak voice: "Bell, you mind fixin' these pillows behind my back? Can't seem to get my breath right."

"I don't mind."

I propped her up with the pillows as best I could, but she still slumped in the bed. Her face was ghostly pale, and she kept letting out heavy sighs.

"Bell, I feel kind of hot. Can you open a window?"

"I don't think that would be good for you, Ms. Emma, 'cause it's a little chilly outside. How 'bout a cool cloth?"

She nodded. I left the room to get a damp cloth. When I returned, she had fallen over slightly. I gently propped her back up and dabbed her face and neck with the cloth.

"That's better," she said, letting out a contented sigh. "I want to talk to you, 'cause I don't believe I have much time left."

"What is it, Ms. Emma?"

"My conscious been bothering me. I want to beg yo' pardon fo' the way I treated you," she whispered.

"I forgive you, but please don't weary yourself with talk. Try to rest some, you're mighty weak."

"Naw, Bell, I gots to get this out of me. You's a right good wife to Buck. And you been better to me than my own chil'ren. I guess what I'm trying to say is...is...is *thank you.*"

The words sounded so strange. That was the first time I had ever heard her say 'em, but I know'd she meant it.

She started going into one of her coughing fits. Between coughs, she asked me to bring her a glass of water. When I came back, she had stopped coughing. I handed her the water, and she grasp the glass with trembling hands. I held the bottom of the glass, to keep it from dropping, and I kept the straw steady enough for her to take a sip.

The words came out a little easier, "Thank you, Bell, thank you."

I placed the glass on the nightstand, and Ms. Emma reached for my hand. I held her cold hand, 'til it went limp in mine. Her eyes became set: not focused on a thing. Her head slowly slumped to the left, 'til her chin rested on her collarbone. It was all over. Ms. Emma was gone.

Chapter 28

Our Grief

Grief clinched my heart after Grandma's words. Silence filled the room. We all needed time to absorb the death of great-grandma Steele. Although it happened over twenty years ago, that night was reiterated.

Grandma seemed to relive those last moments, too. Her speech became weighty. "Yeah...the last whisper of time knocked at the gates of eternity for Ms. Emma."

It felt like a black shadow hovered overhead. I was hoping someone would do something to break the eeriness.

Cherie responded to my inner request. "Grandma, out of all the pictures I've seen of great-grandma Steele, I would have never guessed that she was the way you described her to be." Cherie's voice turned into a whisper. "I used to think it was a compliment when I was told how much I looked like her. I don't take it as a compliment now...not at all."

I waited for Pat to use that opportunity to say something smart. She remained quiet, like the rest of us.

"Baby, it's a lot more to a person than what you see in a picture," Grandma said. "I'm sure you've heard the saying, a picture's worth a thousand words. Well, in this case, a picture hides a lifetime of sorrow."

Cherie's face looked like she was going to lose her composure for sure.

"Keep in mind this one thing, baby, you don't have to make the mistake to learn from it. Don't worry, your life ain't carved in stone—you got time to make changes."

Grandma's comforting eyes brought cheerfulness back into the room. Cherie gave Grandma her warm, loving smile. The smile I had almost forgotten.

Chapter 29

Grandma's Story (The Confession)

Ms. Emma was a thorn in my flesh for years, but I couldn't help but miss her 'round there. I sorted through her things—remembering.

Buck was a pitiful sight. He closed the store for 'bout three weeks. He stayed shut in, hovering over that box that had the picture of Ethel in it. I guess he added his mama's memory to it, too.

Bill came to visit more often, checking on us. He seemed pleased just to sit with Mr. Silas.

Course the other brothers and sisters came 'round for a while. They paid their respects. They'd sit 'round and talk to me 'bout the portion of their mama they had missed all them years. Most of it was misery, but I spared them of that. Like always, the visiting soon stopped.

Mr. Silas was the worst of all. He couldn't seem to stand the sight of anything that reminded him of his wife. Sometimes he wouldn't come out of his room for days. I sent his food to him by the chil'ren. The plates came back half-eaten.

One day, I heard low moans coming from his room. I rushed down the hall and knocked. "Mr. Silas, are you all right?"

He didn't answer, just kept moaning like a wounded animal. I figured I'd better go in to see if I could calm him in some way. I eased the door open and peeked in. He was sitting up in bed with his head in his hands, shaking and crying. I moved closer to the bed.

"Is there anything I can do for you, Mr. Silas?"

He looked up real slow. For the first time, he stared at me for a long while—dead in the eyes.

"Oh my God! Ethel, you done came back," he said, trembling.

"Sir? I'm Bell."

"Ethel, don't call me *suh*...I know that's you...I know them eyes anywhere."

He went into a crying fit all over again.

"Mr. Silas—"

"No, no, no, child...you don't have to call me Mr. Silas no mo'...call me daddy, like you should...I was wrong....so wrong for how I treated you."

I was all confused. Mr. Silas kept on talking out of his head. "You always was a sweet child. I was a fool for making a difference between you and the rest of the fambly...should've treated you better...know'd I should've. I was foolish, foolish, foolish...cared too much 'bout color than my own child."

Mr. Silas let out a loud wail that sent chills through me. "The doctors told me and yo' mama that you had a weak heart. Said we had to treat you with special care. But I didn't listen. That didn't stop me. I know'd better than to make you eat separate from the rest of us. I'm sorry for hurting yo' weak little heart all them years, Ethel."

"Mr. Silas, you're talking out of your head," I said, trying to calm him down.

"It's daddy, it's daddy! I ruined you, gal. Emma tried to warn me 'bout myself. I wouldn't listen to her either. Ever' time I hurt you, I know'd I hurt Buck. 'Specially with...with y'all being...being *twins*. Only difference between y'all was yo' color—dark like mines."

Mr. Silas looked like a madman staring at me. He grabbed my arm and held it tight. "I know'd it won't yo' fault. I was the only dark child my mama had, too. After my Pa died, things changed. People used to make a difference between me and my brothers and sisters—kept saying I won't really my mama's child, 'cause she was half-white. She got so shamed of me, 'til she gave me away—let my grandmama raise me. That's when I started hating dark skin."

He let my arm go and hid his face in his hands. "I'm sorry for making you scrub the floor with that little cloth, and tending the animals when the other chil'ren played. I should've never stopped Buck from choppin' wood for you. I worked you and worked you...'til yo'...'til yo'...'til, yo' weak little heart couldn't take no mo'."

Mr. Silas let out another pitiful wail. "I know'd I was the one who...who...k-k-killed you. When they found you laying by the woodpile, I know'd I was the one who'd done it. Now, you done come back for me."

Mr. Silas kept saying he was sorry over and over again and wouldn't stop.

I slowly backed out of the room. My nerves were moving on their own. I stood outside his door and trembled down to the floor. I cried and cried—for Mr. Silas, Ms. Emma, Buck and Ethel.

Chapter 30

Revelation

I looked at Pat, Pat looked at Cherie, and the three of us gaped at each other. I expected to see the same expression on the other family members' faces. I didn't. The revelation was only new to us. Their cast-down eyes gave us the space to express our shock, without too much attention.

Pat broke the silence. "Grandma, was that really true or was he just talking out of his head?"

"Yes, baby, it was true."

"Pa-Pa had a twin sister who was hated by her own father because of her color?" Cherie whispered.

"Yes, baby, that's true," Grandma said.

"Oh, that's awful," Cherie said, with her eyes watering. "How could someone do that to their own child?"

"You wouldn't expect that from family," Pat added.

Cherie's face turned ash white. It didn't seem that Pat directed her statement at Cherie, but it had the same effect.

"Chil'ren, ignorance is blind—can do plenty of damage," Grandma started, "but when your eyes open and you see the truth, mending can be done, if it's not too late." She glanced from Cherie to Pat.

"Great-grandpa Steele must have had a miserable life, with the thoughts of Aunt Ethel haunting him," Cherie said, with her color returning.

"Yeah, he couldn't run forever—it had to come out. Little did I know how much I convicted him," Grandma said. "I wasn't just Bell—I carried the memory of Ethel in my eyes." Grandma's voice trailed off into a faint whisper, leaving eeriness behind.

I couldn't imagine being in a family with such unfair treatment, especially for something completely out of my control. *Two generations of color-struck pride in the Steele family was more than enough. I'm glad Grandma caught it before it reached into another. At least I hoped so.*

Chapter 31

Grandma's Story (Peacemaking)

It took me awhile to get myself together, after learning about Ethel. I gathered enough nerve to tell Buck what his daddy had told me. He fell down limp in our bedroom chair.

"I was always afraid that would happen," he said, with a far-away gaze. "I figured you would find out one day."

Mr. Silas' mind won't right ever since his confessions. At times he would talk with good sense, but most times he just sat in that room shaking and crying. He had started losing more and more weight. Buck called for a doctor to come and check him. All the doctor could find was a bad case of grief.

It won't easy watching Mr. Silas waste away like that. We contacted the fambly to come spend time with him, while there was still some time left. Visiting picked up for a few weeks, then it all stopped again, as usual. Mr. Silas didn't seem happy to see nobody.

He was a right pitiful sight—small enough for me to carry. His voice dropped down to a whisper, and his breathing got to be more troublesome. We did what we could to make him comfortable.

One rainy day, May 16, 1963, Buck had closed the store and sat with his daddy. "You really need to eat something to give yourself a little more strength."

"Don't need no strength," Mr. Silas whispered, "my time's almost out."

"Stop talking like that. You just need a little food

that's all," Buck said. "Bell, do you mind fetching Daddy some soup?"

I figured it was a waste of time, but I did as I was asked. I brought Mr. Silas a small bowl of soup, a few saltines, and a tall glass of water. I set the tray on the nightstand near his bed.

Mr. Silas let out a low moan when Buck sat him up. I propped pillows all around him for more support.

"Just take a little," Buck said, holding a spoonful of soup to his daddy's mouth.

Mr. Silas shook his head real slow.

"Why don't you try, Bell?" Buck said. "You're better with dealing with the sick than me."

I was afraid to let Mr. Silas see my eyes again. I didn't want him to confuse me with Ethel in front of Buck. I stood over him, hoping he wouldn't look up.

"What about a lil something to drink?" I said, lifting the glass from the tray. I touched his lips with the straw.

To my surprise, he opened his mouth. He just took a tiny sip, but that seemed to have been all he needed. "Something I want to say…while I's got a lil time left."

"Don't use all your energy talking, Daddy. You need to eat something first," Buck said.

"Naw, Buck, gots to get this off my chest…before I meets my maker."

I could tell Buck didn't like hearing that kind of talk. I didn't care for it either, but it was better than hearing him talk out of his head.

"I know I ain't done right by y'all…'specially you, Eth—, I mean, Bell."

"Daddy, please stop talking," Buck pleaded.

Mr. Silas gave a raspy cough. "I was too bull-headed to listen to anybody. Even after yo'…'yo twin died."

"That's enough," Buck said, shifting in his seat. "That's all in the past."

"Let me talk, Buck. You got mo' wind than me," Mr. Silas whispered.

I put my hand on Buck's shoulder and gave it a little squeeze. He sat back in the chair with his head drooped.

"I was a plumb fool…looking at color all them years," Mr. Silas said. He gave another raspy cough. "Wished I had learned it sooner…before…before I lost ever'thing."

There was a long silence. Mr. Silas' eyes filled up, but he didn't make a sound. Then he spoke: "Bell, I want to beg yo' pardon fo' how I treated you. You's been mighty faithful by this fambly…you taught me something."

Mr. Silas looked up at me—dead in the eyes. "A person's worth lies within…and can't be judged by the color of their skin."

He went into a coughing fit—almost strangling. Buck patted his back, 'til he got hisself together.

"Promise me this one thing, Buck," Mr. Silas said, gasping for breath. His breathing was heavy. Real heavy.

"What, Daddy? What is it?"

"Don't ever…let yo' fambly…get like ours." Mr. Silas took a deep breath. "Don't let a deathbed…be yo'…peacemaker."

His last words were slurred, but understood. He slumped on the pillows with a dreadful moan.

"Daddy, Daddy," Buck said, lifting Mr. Silas up on the pillows. There won't no reply. "Daddy, answer me."

Buck looked long and hard into his daddy's face. "You didn't…you didn't…you didn't leave me did you, Daddy?" He shook Mr. Silas a little, patting his face gently.

Mr. Silas didn't answer. His eyes were set.

"D-a-a-a-a-d-d-d-y-y-y!"

Chapter 32

We're a Family Again

"Good Lord, it seems like I can still hear Buck's pitiful wails now," Grandma said, as one tear trickled down her cheek. I guess she had cried the rest of them out a long time ago.

My heart felt like it had been ripped from my chest. I wanted to scream the pain out. I looked around the room at mirror images of how I felt. I watched the tissue box leave one hand after another, until it finally made its way to me. I grabbed a few tissues and passed it on. Grandma never moved, as the family dried their faces. Her gaze was fixed.

Aunt Jean blew her nose, releasing the tension from the air likewise. My throat finally relaxed and opened up more, allowing me to swallow back my remaining tears.

"Yeah, chil'ren, that's how this fambly came to be. We held that promise from then 'til now," Grandma said.

I finally understood what Pa-Pa's teachings meant. It *was* a promise. *Now we all have to make sure we keep it.* I glanced at Cherie and Pat. They seemed to have understood, too.

It was very late. The family started clearing away the extra chairs we had gathered from the kitchen and dining room. Little murmurs of conversation hummed throughout the house.

"Mama, can I get you anything before I leave," Uncle Mason said, from the doorway of the den.

"No, son, I'm quite all right," Grandma said, getting

up from her rocker. She went into the kitchen to see the family out.

The conversations dwindled down to the squeak of Grandma's kitchen door and the light tap that followed, as it softly closed.

We all lived in walking distance, but Aunt Nettie wanted Cherie, Pat, and me to stick around until she brought her car back. She needed help getting the sleepy, little ones home to bed.

The house was completely quiet, leaving the three of us in the same position we were in when Grandma first began her story: me, squeezed in the middle of Pat and Cherie.

"So, Pat, are you interested in attending Shaw or A and T?" Cherie asked, out of nowhere.

"I haven't decided."

"Well, if you are, I have some information from both schools."

"Really?" Pat said, looking puzzled.

"Yes, I can share it with you if you'd like," Cherie said with a hopeful expression.

"Thanks, maybe I can take a look at it," Pat said, smiling.

My heart felt like it was going to burst with excitement. Cherie and Pat were actually talking *peaceably* with each other. *What could I do to keep it going? What contribution could I add?*

"I'm starting driver's ed. next week," I blurted out, too soon to realize how very irrelevant it was to the conversation.

"Huh?" Cherie said, looking at me like I was an alien from outer space.

Pat's eyes went up into her head. "The joys of a freshman," she said, winking at Cherie.

They both laughed. Of course, I joined them. It felt good being wrapped between the warmth of their humor, even if I was the culprit.

"Now, that's what I like to hear," Grandma yelled from the kitchen, "fambly laughing and talking with each other."

The Real "Bell" and "Buck"

Grandma Doll around age 30

Grandma Doll and Pa-Pa Buck

Photo courtesy of Blount's Photography in Greenville, NC

The Old Home Place
(Mr. Silas & Ms. Emma's Home)

Photo courtesy of Blount's Photography in Greenville, NC

The New Home Place
(This is the house Buck built)

Grandma Doll at age 87

We hope this story serves as an inspiration for you (the reader), as it is a testament to the life of a matriarch in our family. Her exemplary faith, forgiveness, and integrity reached into the depths of our hearts and planted a seed of strength.

Pamela & Joel Tuck

Made in the USA
Charleston, SC
21 January 2011